PAINT MECHANICS HANDBOOK

James Benney

Rocky Ridge Publications

Visit: www.jamesbenney.com

ISBN-13: 978-0-9838480-1-1
ISBN-10: 0983848017

Cover art and layout: Crawshaw Design
Editorial Consultant: Robyn Russell

Rocky Ridge Publications

Printed in the United States of America

TABLE OF CONTENTS

INTRODUCTION

This handbook is designed to instill in the reader an appreciation for the importance of each step of the painting process, with the goal ultimately to produce the best-looking, longest lasting paint job possible.

Although professional painters favor many varying products, techniques, tricks, labor saving devices, and so on and so forth, the practices described herein are basic and accepted by most tradespeople.

Essentially an introduction to the craft of painting, the Paint Mechanics Handbook can benefit the do-it-yourselfer, the homeowner seeking estimates, the building manager, and the apprentice painter.

There is much satisfaction to be derived from a good job, and much grief from a poor one. My hope is that this handbook will help you accomplish the former and avoid the latter.

I became a house painter quite by accident, as have so many. When I was fifteen my friend Mike helped his dad paint their house and he thought we could make some bucks painting houses over the summer. I made a few index cards offering "Student Painters", which I put up in the local Safeway in our little suburb of San Francisco and by god we painted all summer. I made enough money to buy a 1955 Chevy hot rod. The year was 1966.

Seven turbulent years and many different jobs later I was working with disadvantaged kids making $2.25 an hour when one of the people whose house we'd painted called to see if I'd be interested in re-painting it. They could pay me $5 per hour.

Forty years later the rest is history. Their neighbors had a little work that needed to be done. Someone down the street liked what I was doing and from there I never looked back. Painting suited me then, and it still does.

I like the scheduling flexibility having my own business gives me (when it's your own business, you can work whatever seventy hours a week you want). I also like the feeling of accomplishment that comes with maintaining and improving the places we're working on every day, wherever they are.

James Benney
2011

WHY WE PAINT

Painting maintains, protects, and beautifies expensive wood, stucco, and metal surfaces. It extends the useful life of buildings and structures, and improves the ambience of the area around them.

Often we paint because we fell into it through some simple twist of fate, such as, it needed to be done. Many people don't like to paint and prefer to pay someone else to do the necessary work. That's fine too.

Painting provides a sense of accomplishment, and reward for effort that is visible and sublime at the same time. Every day, in fact every hour, we can see the results of our labor. There is satisfaction in this. Knowing our work will shine for years to come is not just a concept, it's a fact.

Every day is different. Every space is different, and done properly, we change it for the better.

Proper painting requires concentration almost to the point of meditation.

To be an effective and productive painter, the painter needs to concentrate on the task at hand and be constantly planning ahead in order to perform the work properly. This is true of all craft-work. If you believe that one of life's goals is to be alive in the moment, painting provides ample and varied opportunities to tune your senses.

There is also the constant danger of exposure to hazardous materials and working conditions, and the challenge of minimizing that exposure to keep the craftsperson alert, on their toes, and in the moment.

Many artists and musicians have made excellent house painters due to their natural attention to detail and flair for the dramatic. Also, they like the flexible schedule that is often possible, which allows them to keep developing their own creative outlets.

Truly professional painters are aware of everything going on around them at all times. They are aware of lighting, draperies, rugs, colors, textures, and the mental and physical concerns of the people who will be living and working in and around that painted space.

In other words "Site psychic!" in tune with the total immediate environment.

They become decorators and designers. Their handling of the job determines if the residual effect is positive or negative. Painting is straight shots of psychological awakening coupled with practical, down to earth work. The work keeps the painter grounded while trying to identify the color senses and decorating concerns of the client.

Painters are involved in construction and remodel projects towards the end when everything is coming together (and apart), often the most hectic and stressful time for all the parties involved. It is in working through this stress and conflict that one becomes a skilled arbiter of life's experiences. We are in the background, and yet we see it all.

Stress? Yes! We've experienced plenty of it. Many times the gifted painter will have to diffuse a tense situation with a practical step-by-step approach to the basic work at hand. A deep comprehension of the real issues at play and the deft handling of them can avert a crisis. By the same token, a poor painter can make a bad situation worse.

There will always be painting needing to be done in our lifetimes. Virtually every building that has ever been painted will be painted again, inside and out. Only a few individuals will pursue the skills required to become true paint mechanics.

OUR ENVIRONMENT

Look around you. Here is our environment, pulsing with life. Everything you can see or sense is having an affect on you, whether conscious or unconscious. A dilapidated building conveys a feeling of decay to a neighborhood. Painting can be part of the solution.

We can do anything we want and make our own reality. Our standard of living compares to the rest of the world quite well. And there are still many things we can do today, right now, to improve our lot in life. Painting is one.

Since we're doing it, we might as well do it right and get some satisfaction out of it and take some pride in it. It's nice to walk away with a positive feeling of accomplishment.

We can improve and enhance the immediate environment, without losing sight of the fact that we are working with chemical coatings that have an impact on air quality and need to be applied carefully and effectively. Proper preparation and quality paints can extend the life of a paint job two or three times, dramatically reducing the amount of material needed to properly care for a room or building.

There is also a physical aspect to painting. Painting involves stretching and bending and moving around like few other craft lifestyles. By paying attention to our bodies while we're concentrating on efficient painting techniques we become limber people, unlike most desk jockeys. It's kind of like practicing yoga. Plus, we work outside a lot.
In this trade, we are all artists. Color mixing situation by situation is an art form. Color placement is an art form. Client management is an art form. We develop skills in all these areas while still able to pursue our other dreams and aspirations. The people skills we learn through painting transfer well to any field of interest.

We make our environment a better place to be.

PAINT MECHANICS PSYCHOLOGY

The art of making everyone comfortable with the painters and the paint job is achieved equally through the use of psychological awareness as painting craftsmanship.

There are many instances in which the psychological balance can be won or lost, most of which can be controlled by the painter. Often, exemplary craftsmanship will swing the balance our way.

Cleaning hardware and washing windows is a good example of part psychology, part craft. A beautifully painted room with dirty windows and old paint on the door and window hardware profoundly detracts from the finished effect.

In a high-end, upscale work environment (everywhere, really), every painter needs to think just like a salesperson at Nordstrom, always ready to provide friendly helpful service, all the while performing the work thoroughly and conscientiously.

There is always more work to be done on every structure, often within the next eight to ten years. Someone will be doing it. In order to get respect for our product and skills we have to leave the job site with everyone pleased with the results.

Professional painters have developed a number of techniques to achieve this end.

Here's what I emphasize:

1. Show up on time or early every day. (This is #1 for a reason.)

2. Keep a notebook with you at all times. Use it to record product needs and customer concerns and solutions.

3. Wear clean painters coveralls, pants and whites every day.

4. Carry a vacuum in at the beginning of the job. Use it.

5. Wash windows inside and out whenever possible. Learn to do excellent window washing.

6. Point out old paint from previous paint jobs on floors, furniture, etc. so that you don't get blamed for it. Clean it up if you can.

7. Immediately clean new paint spatters anywhere on floors, walkways, furniture, etc.

8. Always be aware of anyone's concerns and questions regarding the paint job, and address them expeditiously.

9. Leave no trace of painters every day when you leave if possible. The advantage is entirely psychological. Yours and theirs.

10. On every job, do a better job than has ever been done before.

11. Take pride in your product and daily production.

12. Use clean new drop cloths inside.

13. Bring problems you're having out in the open only if necessary. Do not worry customers needlessly.

14. Keep used paint can labels clean.

15. Use plastic liberally to protect furniture, rugs, floors, walls, or anything else that requires protection.

16. Respect the client and the client's home. Realize that painters are a major disruption to their life. Stay out of their space as much as possible.

17. Ask which sink and toilet is best for the painters to use. Clean them yourself every day!

18. When talking to other workers, keep the conversation on edifying and interesting subjects. You never know who might be overhearing you when you least expect it.

19. Do not inflame a client's religious or political passions!

20. No smoking anywhere around the job site, ever.

21. Never damage or scratch any adjacent surface in any way.
    In other words... don't make new work for which there is no pay.

AVOID IRRITATING THE CLIENT

When you are repainting a house that is occupied by the homeowner, don't take your breaks or lunch inside the house in the living and eating areas. Be discreet or use your vehicle. You are in someone's home, and it annoys people to find that their space has been invaded, and to have to straighten up after someone else, no matter how small the clean-up.

Do not read their newspapers. Do not use their tools, ladders, vacuums, cleaning supplies, drinking glasses or silverware.

Do not use their bathrooms if construction toilets are on the job. Be sure to ascertain which bathroom is best for you to use, or if you should go to the nearest gas station.

Do not place any trash in the homeowner's trashcans or trash baskets. Never take anything out of the refrigerator, or use it yourself. Pack out ALL of your own trash.

If you have to wash up at a sink, make sure to clean up well afterwards. Never use a customer's bath or hand towels.

Don't try to make small talk. Let them come to you. Do not use profanity or vulgar language within earshot of clients, customers, or neighbors who might be offended by this behavior.

Reason: No one will want you around again to do more work. Note: All neighbors are potential clients.

If you damage anything, including plants, try to fix the problem without the client ever knowing about it. That's second best. Best is not making the extra work in the first place. If necessary, point it out before they see it.

Reason: Owners realize that some damage may occur. What they don't expect is to discover it themselves. This makes it look like you were not aware of the problem.

Never smoke in or around someone's home.

Reason: Many people are very smoke sensitive.

Clean oil brushes off-site. Clean latex brushes in customer approved sinks only or take them home and clean them.

Reason: Paint in the ground or storm drains is an environmental disaster and a huge fine if anyone discovers it.

At the end of each day, make sure the shop area is cleaned and well-organized, perhaps even covered up with a dropcloth. Police the entire job, picking up even the smallest scraps of trash, and make sure the doors and windows are locked or well-secured.

Reason: The client likes to feel that you are a responsible and conscientious person.

Perform your job professionally and competently and you will find it much easier to avoid irritating the client.

JOB FOREMAN

The job foreman must be completely capable of doing the entire job or at least must know what will have to be done to get it done. He or she should exude confidence at all times. Somebody has to be in charge.

A foreman must know the Procedures, Policies, and Client Psychology backwards and forwards.

The Dictionary of Terms should be studied regularly and the terminology used liberally. People like to think the painters know what they are talking about.

The job foreman has to determine the skills and weaknesses of every painter on the job and use them accordingly.

He/she must be aware of every aspect of the developing project at all times, and be available to the client to keep them updated and to allay any concerns.

He/she must direct all other painters into tasks that can and will develop momentum and be easily checked for thoroughness.

Develop a conservative color sense, so that your opinion has some value. Know when a combination of colors is working, and when they are not. If a color designer is involved, do not offer your opinion unless asked, and then it's usually best to agree with the color designer.

The job foreman should try to view the job through the eyes of the home-owner-customer they are serving.

While working in rooms with furniture and/or hardwood floors, be careful when moving ladders and tools around. One scratch or gouge can cause trouble, and create more unpaid work!

Do not damage or dirty any surface that you are not getting paid to work on. You will have to fix it or clean it for free.

Look around you. How does the client live day to day? Empathize. Many people are very uptight when spending large sums of money. You may think they are so rich that a few thousand dollars doesn't matter to them one way or the other. Usually you'd be wrong. It matters. If they feel they are getting what they pay for, everything will be fine. But don't expect people to pay Cadillac prices for Chevrolet service.

Case in point: We were working on a rain-delayed fifteen thousand dollar exterior in Piedmont. We were nine thousand dollars into the job. The job was eight weeks old. Christmas was the next week. The job foreman went to the job and removed the shop and all evidence of painters so the customer wouldn't have to look at it through the holidays. He spent one hour. They appreciated the thought. Had we waited for them to complain about the shop, it's quite possible that they would have suggested we wait until spring to finish. But we needed that six thousand dollars of remaining work as soon as we could do it. Now it's still there. One hour of thoughtfulness equals six thousand dollars gross income the next month. Well worth-it.

The foreman and all of the painters must be confident that they are producing the best work possible at all times, in order to build trust with the client. Think ahead to payment dates and production expectations.

All conversation and chit-chat on the jobsite should be geared toward painter and customer enlightenment. No loud, obnoxious, or crude behavior should be tolerated.

Post "wet paint" signs to warn people when a freshly painted surface may be subjected to foot traffic. Keep dogs and cats away from wet paint and the job shop if at all possible. Clean up as you go along.

THE USE OF SEQUENCE AND MOMENTUM

Long term professional painters learn how to do the most work with the least amount of energy. This is essentially just productive good work habits and behavior and includes:
• Physical and mental alertness while on the job.
• Sequential, practical workmanship.

Start and complete each step of the painting process one step at a time:
• Set up the area to be painted
• Cover everything you can.
• Load in and set up a shop area
• Bring everything you will need that day in at one time.
• Remove hardware and put in storage box - do it all at once.
• Wash as needed - do all the washing.
• Sand as needed - do all the sanding.
• Repair as needed - do all the repairs.

Plan the job out in your mind. Determine the best time to get repairs done and primer up, etc. in order to get the job done efficiently.

Sequence and momentum are critical to successful painting. The fewer breaks taken while pursuing each task, the better. When painting windows and trim, for instance, after a couple of hours you start to get in the swing of it and momentum takes over and propels you through the day.

In other words, if you have five windows and doors and you prepare and paint each one separately, going through the five prep steps one door and one window at a time, it will take twice as long as if you performed the job in complete sequences. Same job, same end result, one half the work to do it methodically using sequence and momentum.

Similarly, the shorter the distance from the paint bucket to the surface being painted, the better. Try to picture two painters painting a multi-light window. One is holding his bucket in front of himself. The brush moves one or two feet between bucket and window. The other painter has his bucket on the floor behind him. The brush and the painter's hand moves six to eight feet from bucket to window. Repeat 50 times. Obviously the first painter doesn't have to work as hard and gets more done!

Performing work in the correct sequence is a great time and energy saver. When you have an extension ladder set up on an exterior, do everything possible from each ladder set. The fewer times you have to move the ladder into that position, the better. It's less work. It has to do with approaching every step in an organized fashion.

Completing each sequence or section is also important for no other reason than to be able to look back and say "that's done" and it looks sharp. That enhances both yours and the client's feelings of accomplishment!

COLOR MANAGEMENT- ON THE JOB

Helping the client with color can be one of the most costly propositions we partake in due to the extra time spent mixing colors, putting up samples, and so on and so forth.

Even professional color designers often mistakenly pick colors that the client simply doesn't like when they are up on the wall.

To minimize this disruption, we have fine print on the back of our estimates that states that colors will be chosen in advance, or we get paid time and materials to work on them on site.

Rarely does either of these conditions occur automatically.

People want our opinions because they know we are in the business and are working with color every day, and they are right. Painters routinely doing custom high-end work often are very familiar with contemporary color trends and pleasing decorative effects.

Only one person should work with the client on color decisions.

When a decorator or color designer is involved, they are always right as far as we are concerned.

Still, it is best to learn some basic, conservative color sense, and trust your instincts. But be sure you know how much time you're getting paid for and how much you are not.

We can help clients come up with nice colors, and usually relatively inexpensively when compared to decorator's prices. However, if our help is not well-defined, and it turns into an hour-after-hour proposition due to multiple attempts at getting the "right" color, we often wind up paying for it. Only rarely can we afford it.

LOAD IN AND SET UP SHOP

The first few hours of direct, on-the-job contact with the client are the most important, and will help to determine the ease or difficulty of customer relations throughout the job.

A good first impression will usually take the edge off the client's fear that they will be dealing with typical painters, i.e. messy, surly, loud, obnoxious workers. Anything that we do that reinforces their fears of these stereotypes will make the job harder to complete with 100% customer satisfaction.

Therefore, it is always important (particularly on the first day) to:

1. arrive a little early.
2. be especially clean and neat in appearance.
3. assess the scope of the job with the client.
4. carefully remove impediments (furniture, rugs, etc.)
5. find the best location to set up a shop.
6. always keep in mind that we are disrupting the life of the client, and anything we do to minimize that disruption will be appreciated.
7. when starting interior jobs, it never hurts to carry a vacuum into the house when you first arrive. This always impresses the client.
8. set up your shop.
9. make a note of old paint on floors and fixtures or other surfaces that are somehow already damaged and point them out. This will prevent our being blamed for these when the job is over.

The job site shop should be out of your way and out of the customer's way. Do not set up near furnaces, water heaters, or stoves (fire hazard). When setting up on interior floors and rugs, lay a piece of six-mil plastic down under the dropcloth to prevent accidental soaking through of spilled paint or thinner. Bring in the tools you will need that day. Keep the shop clean and well-organized. Unused dropcloths should be kept neatly folded.

While loading in tools, ladders and dropcloths, be very careful not to bang, scratch, or ding adjoining doors, casings, and walls. One mistake here will cost us to repair and repaint a surface that we aren't getting paid for.

Once load in and set up are completed, work may begin according to the defined procedures.

CLEAN UP AND LOAD OUT

Remember that the customer will be very concerned about any new paint, scrapes, or stains on their floors, rugs, walkways, decks, furniture or fixtures. When these do occur, try to clean them up before the customer notices them. This will save you from having them constantly looking over your shoulder to make sure you don't do it again.

Clean up of the job site should be ongoing and complete. Proper finish painting always takes place in a clean environment. Garbage and unnecessary tools or equipment should be loaded out when they are no longer needed.

As the job begins and progresses, it is important to clean up thoroughly following preparation of the surfaces. Debris from prep procedures can be tracked into adjoining rooms or damage floors under the dropcloths.

Dust can travel a long way during preparation, and efforts should be made to contain it in the area where work is proceeding. Tape two-mil plastic over open doorways when necessary, and remove it after clean up. Tape carefully to the sides and tops of door casings, and as lightly as possible to walls to prevent the tape from pulling off old paint when it is removed. Use blue light-adhesive tape.

Even though dropcloths are always used, paint spatters or splatters on drops can be a problem and should always be wiped up immediately to prevent tracking into their adjoining areas or possibly having them soak through the dropcloth and staining the floor or rug beneath.

Load out carefully and efficiently. Carry as much out to the truck each time as you safely can. Remember to use caution to protect adjacent surfaces. Leave the job site clean and tidy every time.

Dispose of dry waste off site. Used paint cans can be included in dry waste if they have been brushed out and are dry. Wet waste (solvents, extra paint, etc.) must be disposed of according to your state's waste management rules and regulations. Often thinner can be reused and paint can be donated to charity.

SUBJECTIVE JUDGMENTS

There are many instances in the course of a paint job that require quick decision making on many levels relating to expectations, jobsite conditions, and practical paths to job completion.

Removing Hardware

Hardware removal requires a situation-by-situation judgment call on the part of the estimator/painter. High-end jobs require the most hardware removal.

Important! Make a note of any missing hardware or screws immediately upon discovery. We must have proof that we did not lose them. Similarly, during the hardware removal process, it is always advisable to make a note of old paint spatters on floors, scratched window glass, gouges in floors, dinged furniture, etc., because many times the customer will never have noticed these items until after the job is done, and then will associate them with our job. Carry a notebook at all times. Use it!

Interior Washing

Judgment is often called into play when preparing to wash. How dirty is it and how clean does it need to be are questions that must be answered on-site by the foreman. The objective is to paint a surface that will allow for secure long-term adhesion of new paint to old paint. The difference is not apparent upon completion of the job.
It is in the future that the benefits of careful washing can be observed.

Our standard procedure is to wash and sand all trim and entire kitchen and baths. Then there is no doubt that our paint will stick to that surface permanently.

Opening Stuck Windows

If windows get stuck as a result of our paint job, we are responsible for making them work. This is good example of making work that we don't get paid for.

It is important that the job foreman be fully aware of all windows that were painted shut previously. We will charge extra to open these windows, if it is necessary.

A FEW IMPORTANT SUGGESTIONS

1. Always have the following items on you at all times while painting:
    A clean rag
    Putty knife (2" flexible blade)
    Duster brush
    Sandpaper squares (80 grit & 180 grit)
    Swiss army knife
    A notebook and pen

2. Do not leave open paint cans or buckets in heavily trafficked areas,
    or in any place where they could be easily knocked over.
    Reason: Paint spills are a mess.

3. Always cover your paint bucket with a rag when not in use, with the
    brush in it, and set it in a shady, cool place away from foot traffic.
    *Reason: An uncovered brush will harden very quickly, and dirt and debris
    can blow into the material.*

4. On interior jobs, always cover furniture with clean, light-weight
    two-mil plastic.
    *Reason: Dropcloths are often dirty and dusty. They are also
    abrasive and can scratch fine finishes.*

5. Never place wet rags or sponges on any surface except inside a pail
    or sink.
    *Reason: Wet rags or sponges can be the cause of expensive
    furniture or floor refinishing projects.*

6. Do not wear work boots with Vibram soles when working inside.
    Reason: This type of lugged sole leaves black marks on floors.

7. Avoid painting in temperatures below 50 degrees, and in direct hot
    sunlight.
    *Reason: Paint will not dry properly below 50 degrees, and can dry
    too fast in direct sunlight and will not adhere as well as it should.*

8. Avoid painting with exterior latex paint on the outside of a house too

late in the day on cold winter days.
Reason: The evening dew will dissolve the still-damp paint and cause it to run, sag, or blush overnight.

9. Always pour paint from the back side of the paint can.
    Reason: Dried paint on the front of the can will obscure the label.

10. Always wipe out the rim of the paint can with a brush before replacing the lid, even if the lid is not to be sealed down right away.
    Reason: This prevents paint build-up, which makes for a poor seal that is not air-tight. A skin will then form on the surface of the paint.

11. At the end of each day, make sure the shop area is cleaned and well-organized, perhaps even covered up with a dropcloth.
    Reason: Everyone will feel better about everything.

LADDERS AND LADDER SAFETY

TYPES OF LADDERS

Generally speaking, only three types of ladders are used in painting: Step ladders, extension ladders, and combination ladders. Most ladders are constructed of aluminum because they are lighter and easier to move around quickly, and can be stored outside on job sites that are exposed to the elements without the concern that rot may weaken the rungs of the wood ladders. Fiberglass ladders are popular because they don't conduct electricity and can be used without danger of shock around power lines.

Stepladders: A stepladder is a portable, self-supporting ladder, which is not adjustable in length. A stepladder has flat steps, a hinged back and a shelf upon which one may rest a paint can or bucket. This shelf is definitely not to stand or step on. Never walk away from a stepladder with a paint can, electric sander, or any tool sitting on the ladder shelf. Stepladder size is determined by measuring the overall length of the ladder along the front edge of the side rails. All stepladders are equipped with steel safety spreaders, designed to prevent the ladder from suddenly closing. Always make sure the spreaders are "locked" before using the ladder, and that all four feet are firmly on the ground.

Extension Ladders: An extension ladder consists of two or more sections arranged to permit adjustment of length. The size of an extension ladder is indicated by the sum of the lengths of the sections. This means that a twenty-four foot ladder is made of two twelve foot sections, but the maximum extended length is twenty-one feet. High grade rope and pulleys are used for raising the upper section. Extension ladders are equipped with automatic locks. Be certain that both locks are fully engaged before ascending the ladder. Some ladders are equipped with adjustable self-leveling feet for use on uneven terrain. Always visually check to make sure the feet are locked before ascending. When resting a ladder against a wall, place the base of the ladder out from the wall at a distance that is approximately one fourth the total extended length of the ladder.

Combination Ladders: A combination ladder, also called a 5-way or stairway ladder, is a ladder which can be set up as either a short extension ladder, or as a stepladder. This ladder can be set up as a stepladder on a stairway to conform to the rise of the stairs. Caution should be used when this ladder is set up in stepladder configuration. The extension section is not flared at the base like the stepladder section, causing the ladder to not be as stable as a regular stepladder of the same height.

LADDER DO'S AND DON'TS

Be aware that falls from ladders are the #1 cause of workplace injuries. Any extension ladder angle under 75 degrees requires special footing, and any angle over 75 degrees to vertical requires lashing the tip of the ladder to the structure in an approved manner so it can be described as a "fixed" ladder.

1. Be sure to anchor the ladder feet securely on slippery surfaces.

2. Always face the ladder while climbing up or down. Keep both hands free for climbing whenever possible.

3. Never stand a ladder on loose or wet soil without first placing a good broad platform of wood under the feet so they cannot sink.

4. Be sure your shoes and the ladder rungs are free of oil, grease or mud.

5. When working on a ladder, do not lean too far back or to the side. No matter how tempting it is, don't stretch too far trying to reach that last six inches. Stretching may save the couple of minutes it takes to move the ladder, but at the risk of a serious injury, it is not worth it.

6. The top of a stepladder should not be used as a step.

7. Do not splice together two short ladders to make a long section.

8. If a ladder stands in front of a doorway, and could be jarred by some one opening the door, lock the door or have someone guard it. Automatic garage door openers, activated by the unwary, have toppled many a painter.

9. To prevent ladder marks on a wall, install ladder gloves onto the top section of the extension ladder. Remove these gloves when transporting the ladder.

10. Wood ladders should not be painted. They should be kept coated with clear Spar Varnish so the grain structure of the ladder will be visible at all times.

11. Do not use ladders for guys, skids, or any purpose other than for which they were intended. Ladders are not substitutes for ramps or stairways. Extension ladders should not be used as planks by laying them level and placing a board or plywood on top of them.

12. Be sure all four feet of stepladders are secure on the ground before using. Stepladders not secured this way have been known to start "walking" by themselves when the painter is working up near the top of the ladder. Many injuries have resulted from this occurring unexpectedly.

13. If ladder jacks and planks are in use, every person working on the plank must be aware of OSHA safety regulations regarding such use.

14. Ladders providing access to roofs or gables must be tied down securely before use. Painters working on high roof sections must wear a safety belt tied to a rope that will keep them from falling in the event of ladder slippage, earthquake, or medical emergency.

LADDER REMINDERS

— Be sure all of your ladders are sound, strong, and in good condition for safe use. Never borrow or use a ladder that does not belong to you.

— All ladders must be removed from the working area at the end of the day and placed in a secure place. This will prevent children from playing and perhaps injuring themselves on ladders. It will also reduce the risk of thievery.

— Ladders are to be tied upon truck racks according to an approved method demonstrated by the foreman. NEVER LEAVE LADDERS ON A TRUCK OR VAN RACK THAT ARE NOT TIED DOWN because a forgetful driver could cause serious roadway problems.

— When untying a ladder from a truck rack, always remove it at once. If two ladders are lashed together on the rack, and only one removed, always remove the other at once, or tie it back down on the rack.

— When ladders are loaded onto the truck at the end of the job, do not stack some ladders on the truck at one time (untied), then stack more ladders on later. Perform the whole operation at one time, and tie them down. This prevents someone from driving away, assuming that the ladders have been secured.

— Remember to THINK SAFETY and PRACTICE SAFETY at all times.

PRACTICAL POLICIES

Work Assignments

It is recognized that absences, shortages of materials and supplies, equipment breakdowns, rush orders, sudden changes in work loads, etc., frequently necessitate assigning people to different tasks on short notice. A Paint Mechanic should be ready for work wherever and whenever at all times.

Weather conditions or unusual job demands sometimes necessitate abnormal work schedules.

Radios

Radios are seldom permitted on job-sites. Paint Mechanics are expected to focus their attention on the work at hand at all times.

Tool Grip - Paint Mechanic Ready For Work

The purpose of the hand tool grip is to provide the painter with immediate access to frequently used tools. Every painter should bring their grip with them every day, and to always keep it readily accessible. Each painter is expected to use the tools from their own grip.

Lost or broken tools must be promptly replaced.

Smoking

Smoking is discouraged for safety reasons, due to the presence of flammable solvents, and the ever-present danger of fires caused by cigarette butts that are not properly extinguished. Nowadays many people are simply repulsed by the smell of cigarette smoke anywhere.

Illness

Paint Mechanics who become ill during working hours should leave work. This is a safety issue. When not fully engaged and attentive, accidents happen.

Dress Code

Paint Mechanics should wear fresh, clean coverall whites each day. A spare set of whites should be carried by each painter at all times, in the event of paint spills, etc.

Work boots should be worn. (Non-scuff).

Garments should be loose enough to be comfortable. Wearing of painters' hats is encouraged.

Courtesy

Paint Mechanics should try to avoid working in a manner that obstructs or hinders other tradesmen or homeowners from completing necessary tasks.

Suggestions

It is important to maintain an open mind in regards to the improvement of any and all operating procedures, and to encourage everyone to make suggestions to this end. Suggestions are welcomed on such subjects as safety, and ways to save on labor, money, energy, time, and materials.

Automobiles

Messy oil or fluid leaks from painter's trucks and cars are not overlooked by the company or our customers. When this condition is occurring, care should be taken with regard to protecting driveways and streets near our work-sites.

COST CONTROL

One of the major responsibilities of all Paint Mechanics is to help keep costs down. This can be accomplished by keeping the following in mind:

1. Carefully study every potential chance of waste on the job and plan concrete actions to eliminate waste of time and materials. Everyone has a responsibility to correct identified deficiencies.

2. Constantly search for ways to improve work performed. Each major job and function should be analyzed so that ways for improving performance can be identified and implemented. Look for ways to save materials, and most importantly, TIME, in the performance of the job.

3. Follow the code of safety procedures in order to reduce the chance of accidents.

4. Arrange work schedules and job procedures in such a way that everyone can perform their specified tasks with as little wasted effort and backtracking as possible.

5. Inspect equipment, tools, and supplies to guarantee that they are in good working condition. If equipment does not function efficiently, time is lost, performance is not up to standards, and costs increase.

6. Experienced painters should oversee the work, and be sure every one understands their jobs and knows exactly what they are expected to do. Help the new people.

7. Evaluate the use of equipment and machines to see that the most efficient and economical procedures are used.

8. Everyone should be encouraged to make suggestions on improving job performance and reducing waste and costs.

TOOL AND BRUSH MAINTENANCE

All tools should be kept clean and ready to use.

Proper care of brushes and rollers will vary somewhat from individual to individual. Some painters clean and dry their brushes and rollers every day. Others argue that the labor and material cost of cleaning daily is more expensive than buying new brushes and rollers more frequently.

In the case of cleaning roller covers used in oil base paint, it has been generally accepted for many years that it is better by far to throw away the cover than to attempt to clean it. This is often the case with latex roller covers as well.

During a job we will wrap a cover in plastic to keep it wet if we will be using that paint again. Otherwise, we usually knife the paint out of them and toss them. If an apprentice is available, we will occasionally have them clean latex covers. Journeyman painters with three or more years experience are too valuable to waste their time cleaning a $3 roller cover.

Latex brushes should be cleaned thoroughly every day with warm water and soap, and laid out carefully to dry. Some exterior latex paints are alkyd/oil modified. Brushes used with these products must be quick rinsed in paint thinner after they have been cleaned with soap and water. Sometimes, especially outside in warm weather, a brush needs to be cleaned once or twice during the day to prevent paint from caking and drying near the heel.

Oil brushes in particular must be carefully maintained to prolong their use-fulness. Many painters will clean and dry these brushes daily. Proper cleaning of oil brushes requires a vigorous rinse in paint thinner combined with combing paint from the heel, followed by spinning out the bristles. This process is then repeated two or three times in clean thinner.

It is important not to waste thinner during these procedures for two reasons:

1. thinner is expensive.
2. disposing of used thinner is very expensive.

After oil brushes have been cleaned, and spun free of thinner, replace them in their jackets immediately. Nylon brushes should be dried before replacing in jackets.

Other painters will go through step 1 of the above, then leave the brush soaking overnight in clean thinner, and spin it out in the morning before beginning work. When brushes of any kind are left soaking like this, they should be in a bucket or can that is tilted slightly to ease the pressure on the tips of the bristles, or they should be suspended in the bucket or can. The thinner level should come just up to the heel of the brush (where bristle meets ferrule).

Some painters will leave their brush soaking in paint overnight. This will shorten the life of the brush considerably, but in some situations this drawback is offset by the added time the painter has to get the paint up on the wall, so to speak.

Brushes must be in good condition to achieve maximum productivity. They should be replaced as soon as their efficiency is impaired. Old brushes can be used for some stain or stucco jobs, or as dusters.

RISK CONTROL PROGRAM

As a Paint Mechanic, you accept an ethical obligation to your fellow painters and/or clientele to see that operations under your care and control are carried out in an efficient and safe manner.

Along with other responsibilities, safety awareness must always exist in your thinking and planning. Because of this, you must prevent obvious unsafe acts on the part of those you work with, and you must also anticipate potential hazards.

After an accident occurs, it is too late to prevent it. All painters must recognize that working in an unsafe manner is counterproductive. Most importantly, each painter is encouraged to demonstrate leadership ability by setting a good example.

Paint Mechanics have the responsibility to enhance the safety program. To do this, safety must become a part of the job function along with the following responsibilities:

1. Be familiar with the safety program and ensure its effective implementation.
2. Be aware of all safety considerations when introducing a new process, procedure, machine or material to the workplace.
3. Give maximum support to all programs and committees whose function is to promote safety and health.
4. Wear appropriate safety equipment as required.
5. Review all accidents and near-misses to ensure that appropriate actions are taken to prevent repetition.
6. Correct any Safety Hazard that has been identified in a timely manner.

We expect all Paint Mechanics to be safety-conscious and to assist us in identifying conditions at our job sites that might cause an accident.

1. Every Paint Mechanic should maintain a first aid kit in their vehicle.
2. Safety glasses should always be available.
3. Rubber gloves should always be available.

4. Dust masks should always be available.
5. An approved respirator should always be available.

Horseplay

Horseplay and practical joking can result in serious injuries or death. Refrain from it at all times, and encourage your crew to do so as well.

Housekeeping

1. A clean work area makes for a safer as well as a more pleasant place to work. Everyone is expected to help keep the surroundings as neat and orderly as possible.
2. Trash receptacles are to be located on the job site. Place all litter from lunches, scrap materials, etc. in these receptacles.
3. Be health, safety, and fire prevention conscious.

Personal Hygiene

1. Wash hands thoroughly before eating or smoking (after work).
2. Change clothes at the end of the day when working on jobs with heavy particulate exposure, i.e. scraping and sanding.

All OHSA regulations must be adhered to and the following are to be noted:

1. Common sense is the most important safety rule of all. Please use it at all times.
2. Be careful with your hands and hair when operating machinery.
3. All machinery must be turned off when not in use or unattended.
4. If an operation calls for more than one person, the required persons must be present before starting that operation.
5. Machinery must be turned off before cleaning, clearing jams, or making repairs. Machines must be unplugged before working on any electrical parts.
6. Operating shortcuts are not to be taken.

Knee Pads

Should be worn when a painter's weight is stressed on their knees, at their discretion.

Goggles

Goggles are required when working on jobs that require eye protection, i.e. using grinders, disc sanders, sandblasters, and performing overhead prep.

Gloves

To be worn at all times when there is potential hand or finger danger.

SAFETY RULES

For the protection and safety of all painters, Paint Mechanics has established the following rules designed to prevent accidents and injuries:

1. Proper footwear and clothing will be worn at all times.

2. Do not wear loose clothing, jewelry or keep long hair in a position where there is a danger of catching such articles in moving machinery.

3. Horseplay, running, fighting or any activity that may result in injury or accident should not be tolerated.

4. Eye protection is required when performing any task that could produce flying particles.

5. Operate machinery with all guards in place. Do not tamper with safety devices.

6. Do not operate any machine you are not familiar with.

7. Machines must never be cleaned, adjusted or repaired until after the machine is turned off, the circuit broken at the power source (including lock-out) and a warning tag is placed at the controls.

8. Do not leave tools, materials or other objects on the floor that might cause others to trip and fall.

9. Do not block exits, fire doors, aisles, fire extinguishers, gas meters, electrical panels or traffic lanes.

10. Avoid risk of rupture, internal injury or back injury in attempting to lift or push excessive loads. If an object is too heavy to move without strain, ASK FOR HELP.

11. Observe the correct position for lifting: Stand with your feet slightly apart, assume a squatting position with knees bent and tuck your chin. Tilt head forward, grasp the load with both hands and gradually push up with your legs, keeping your back straight and avoiding any abrupt movement.

12. Do not distract others while working. When approaching a machine operator or a concentrating painter for any purpose, do so from the front or the side in a way that he or she will see you coming and will not be shocked or surprised. If conversation is necessary, first make sure any machine is turned off.

13. Do not allow oil, wax, water, paint, or any other materials to remain on the floor where you or others may slip.

14. When handling hazardous materials be sure you follow prescribed safety procedures and use required safety equipment. When using secondary containers filled by others, ensure that they are labeled as to their contents and hazards.

15. Use appropriate gloves when handling materials with sharp or jagged edges, which may result in lacerations.

16. Unnecessary and excessive haste is the cause of many accidents. Exercise caution at all times. WALK, DO NOT RUN!

17. The use of hot production equipment or materials for the purpose of cooking or heating food is strictly prohibited.
It is imperative that all painters be thoroughly familiar with the above safety rules.

SAFETY REMINDERS

1. Never leave solvent-soaked or oily rags sitting in a pile.

Reason: Fire hazard. Chemical reactions will raise the temperature of the rags and can result in spontaneous combustion. Always place all such rags in a bucket of water.

2. Always wear rubber gloves when washing with TSP solution, even for a short time.
   Reason: The TSP solution will not seem caustic at first, but by the time you feel it, your hands will be burned.

3. Never leave the caps off of solvent cans at any time.
   Reason: Accidental spills and fire hazard.

4. Always wear safety goggles or a face shield when using a disc sander or grinder.
   Reason: These tools are driving abrasives and steel filings at high speed toward your eyes.

5. Don't leave an electric sander sitting on a step ladder.
   Reason: It's possible that someone will walk by, trip on the electric cord, and pull the sander off the shelf, damaging the sander and/or that person, and who knows what else.

HAZARDOUS COMMUNICATION PROGRAM

All Paint Mechanics are expected to be aware of workplace exposure to hazardous materials in the painting business. We work with oil base paints, mineral spirits, paint removers, and particulates in the air.

Proper handling of these materials and appropriate protections are important aspects of the painting trade.
Always read the label on any unfamiliar product before using. Dispose of hazardous waste by approved methods as required by law.

FIRES

1. All Paint Mechanics should know the OSHA standards pertaining to fire prevention and fire hazards, and should see that they are complied with.

2. Precautions - Store all rags or paper towels that are soaked in solvents (or linseed oil, varnish oil or similar products) in a bucket of water until they can be disposed of properly.

3. Fire extinguishers of an approved type and size should be on hand at all work sites.

4. Precautions taken when removing paint by burning with a torch:
   A. Hose down all surfaces adjacent to the working area. This includes the roof, the ground, and any other nearby surface which could catch fire.
   B. Always have a garden hose (with a trigger-type nozzle attached) turned on and within reach.
   C. Never leave a torch turned on without using, or leave torches unattended.
   D. Complete all burning operations two hours before leaving the job site each day.
   E. At the end of each day, clean up all burned debris, and place in a fireproof container or bucket of water.

IN CASE OF FIRE

KEEP CALM

1. Remove all persons from the fire area.
2. Notify the Fire Department - dial 911.
3. Close all doors and windows in the fire area, ONLY if this can be done safely.

The person reporting the fire to the fire department should provide them with the following information:

1. Name
2. Address
3. What is burning (machines, paper, etc.)
4. Location of fire
5. Type of fire (electrical, liquid, etc.)

Additional assignments:

1. Attempt to extinguish the fire with the use of on-premise equipment (extinguishers, hoses, etc.) A minimum of two persons is required to fight a fire. To ensure safety, this is to be done only during the early stages of the fire.
2. Clear area of debris.
3. Close all doors and windows.
4. Check driveways to see they are clear for entry of fire fighting equipment. See that gates are unlocked and open.
5. Wait at front entrance for arrival of fire department. Direct firemen to the fire if necessary.

Re-entry onto the property will not be permitted until it is declared safe to do so by the local fire/law enforcement officials.

EMERGENCY ACTION PLAN

Major disasters including fires, floods, hurricanes, earthquakes, and acts of God must be anticipated and procedures have been developed to protect the well-being of our personnel and our community.

The following outlines emergency measures to be taken in the event of a fire or other emergency.

Remember, your conduct and actions during the first few minutes of any emergency may not only save your life, but the lives of your fellow workers and other members of the community as well.

GENERAL INFORMATION

Do Not Panic.

Contact 911 for any of the following reasons:

1. Fire or disabling accident on the jobsite.
2. Any external hazardous condition on or near jobsite.

PAINTER RESPONSIBILITIES

1. Discus an emergency evacuation plan.
2. Make certain the program is familiar to all personnel and that all new painters are promptly oriented.
3. Periodically check with painters to be sure that they are familiar with procedures in case of fire.
6. Be sure all personnel are familiar with and make thorough fire prevention inspections.
7. Take necessary steps required to correct any fire hazards discovered.

INTERIOR

PROCEDURES

REMOVE HARDWARE

Normally it is advisable to remove all electrical switch plates, doorknobs and latch hardware, and window latches. The purpose is to get them out of the way while prepping and painting, and to clean and replace them following painting. If the door latch hardware is not removed and there is a chance that the door could shut, it is advisable to put the knob mechanism back on so that no one gets trapped in a room.

Only under maximum high-end conditions are hinges removed. Removing hinges from cabinet doors and shutters requires numbering each cabinet door or shutter while they are being taken down so that they can be put back exactly as before. Use a screwdriver to inscribe roman numerals on the underside or top edge, out of sight.

Care must be taken that not a single screw is misplaced during this process. Hardware should be placed in a solid box or container, one for each room, clearly labeled. Some rooms will have an extraordinary amount of hardware. It is advisable in that case to attach the screws with masking tape to each individual piece of hardware, in order to eliminate time- consuming sorting of screws at the end of the job.

Good screwdrivers are required. Screwdrivers are to be used for removing and replacing screws only. They are not to be used to open paint cans or as chisels, etc. This will dull the tip and eventually damage screw slots. Always use the right size screwdriver to match the screw head. Stripped screw heads prolong both removal and replacement. Occasionally, there will be a piece of hardware that is so difficult to get off that it is faster to clean it in place and paint around it. This is a judgment call. Seriously stripped screw heads on hardware that must be removed can be drilled out, carefully.

Paint Mechanics should always be extremely security conscious. Door and window latches on the ground floor should be replaced daily. Often, alarm systems are involved, even on the second floor. These areas must be secured so that wind gusts don't blow open a window and set off the alarm.

Do not attempt to remove alarm system electrical covers. Work around them.

Unpainted heater and vent covers in the walls should also be removed. Closet door pop-out handles and clothes hooks inside closets should be removed.

When working on double hung windows, leave the latch secured and re-move the back piece first. It is easier to keep the window stable when it is latched.

Curtain hardware can be left in place unless it is going to be eliminated. Occasionally, it is simpler to take it off before painting, but not often.

When possible, leave light fixtures in place, or only loosen the screws. If removal is necessary, carefully check to be sure that the electricity is off, and mark hot wires to facilitate replacement. Poor electrical work can cause a fire or injury. Be careful, especially in old buildings.

Front door hardware can be tricky, and should only be removed as needed. Some mechanisms require a locksmith to be put back together.

Previously painted hardware is sometimes simply repainted. Other times it is removed, cleaned with paint remover and replaced after painting. When old paint has clogged screw heads on a piece of hardware to be removed, the best approach is to use an artist brush and a capful of paint remover, and dab a little on each affected screw head. This will soften the paint enough to allow the screwdriver to get a good grip on the head. A faster approach is simply to carefully scrape the dried paint out of the slot with the corner of a putty knife. Remember, do not strip the screw head, or scratch the hardware.

Make a note of any missing hardware or screws upon discovery and re-place if possible.

INTERIOR WASHING

Previously painted kitchens, bathrooms, and enameled doors, windows, baseboards, and casings should be cleaned with an appropriate strength trisodium phosphate (TSP) solution, and rinsed thoroughly prior to any preparation or painting. The reason for this is that new paint will not adhere properly to these surfaces under normal conditions due to a several year build-up of furnace residues, cooking greases, and soapy steam films.

Walls and ceilings previously painted with flat latex paints do not usually need to be cleaned, except around light switches. However, in situations involving heavy cigarette, cigar, or pipe smokers, some areas may need to be cleaned to avoid bleed-through of messy nicotine stains. Mildew may need to be treated with a 1/2 bleach, 1/2 water solution to neutralize.

Sanding does not take the place of washing and in some situations can be counterproductive if done without washing first.

Often, the most easily overlooked areas that are not washed become the biggest problems in the future, i.e. baseboards and lower door casings. It is important that all surfaces needing cleaning are done thoroughly, carefully, and completely.

Trisodium phosphate powder can be mixed with water to varying degrees of strength. This will be determined by the condition of the surface to be cleaned.

IMPORTANT! Wear rubber gloves at all times and keep the wash solution off your skin and out of your eyes. Wear goggles when washing ceilings. TSP will permanently spot wood floors immediately upon contact so they must be completely protected along with furniture and rugs.

The tools required for proper cleaning are: Two clean two- gallon or larger buckets for wash water and rinse water; Two clean sponges; rubber gloves; TSP; goggles, and clean rags and dropcloths. Under some conditions in kitchens, due to excessive grease build-up, a six-inch nylon brush is used to brush on a heavy TSP solution and the surface is rinsed twice. Change rinse water frequently. Change TSP wash water when it is too dirty to clean efficiently.

Be careful not to wash any surface outside of the area designated for painting because the new, partially clean surface may contrast with an adjacent dirty surface in an unsightly way.

The objective is to paint a clean surface that will allow for secure long-term adhesion of new paint to old paint. The difference is not apparent upon completion of the job. It is in the future that the benefits of careful washing can be observed.

REPAIR WOODWORK (INTERIOR)

NEW AND RE-DO

Repairs on new woodwork are to be performed after the prime coat is dry. Repairs on re-do's are to be performed after removing the hardware and washing thoroughly.

Generally speaking, open cracks between the woodwork and walls or ceilings should be caulked, filling the crack as deep as possible with the caulk. Similarly, cracks between pieces of trim should be caulked. Fill deep into the crack using a caulk gun. Cut the tip of the tube in a slant with a small or large hole depending on how deep the fills need to be. Use your finger to smooth the caulk. Carry a wet rag to keep your finger clean.

Deep holes can be filled with Fix-All, a fast drying powder and water mixture. Shallow holes can be filled with putty or spackle. If sanding the repair will be necessary, use spackle.

All nail holes, hammer defacements, voids, and other depressions in the surface of the wood are to be filled with a high-quality, non-shrinking, pre-mixed spackling compound. Make sure spackle is smooth and creamy by stirring well and adding a small amount of water if necessary. Spackle that is too dry cannot be driven deep into holes, nor will it float out well over shallow defacements.

Note: Other products may also be used to fill nail holes. Fix-all can be mixed up in small quantities, and has the advantage of drying quickly and actually expanding as it dries, so that it bonds well in deep nail holes and the excess can be sanded off or wiped off with a wet rag when dry. Painter's putty, linseed oil putty and glazing compound will shrink as they dry. Automotive lacquer glazing compounds are durable, waterproof, and pliable, but are slow drying and will shrink as they dry. Automotive lacquer glazing putty, also called spot putty, is quick drying and easy to apply over smooth glossy enamelized surfaces, but it also shrinks as it dries.

Using a flex-blade putty knife, force the spackle deep into nail holes under pressure and knife off the excess from the surface. Holes which are not completely filled on the first application are called "cat's eyes" and must be refilled. Heavy deposits of spackle left around a hole add to the work of the next step in the process, which is the finish sanding. (We call this "making work" that we don't get paid for)

When Fix-all is used to fill nail holes in new wood, wipe with a wet rag or sponge before the Fix-all completely cures (fifteen minutes) and you won't have to sand the residue left over or the slight protruding effect in nail holes that occurs because the fix-all expands as it dries. Never create more work when doing repairs by being sloppy the first time. Do it right, step by step, the FIRST time.

Caulking is always a good way to smooth door and window casings and baseboard joints prior to painting. This makes a clean cut-in line possible. This is especially important when the wall and trim colors are significantly different, and the cut-in line is highly visible. Caulk must be applied under pressure deep into the crack. This will minimize shrinkage as the caulk dries. Remove excess caulk immediately with a wet rag because dried caulk cannot be sanded.

On old woodwork, your judgment will be called upon to assess the extent of repairs required. Normally, eye level woodwork should get more attention than baseboards, for instance. In many cases the construction was sub-standard to begin with, and does not merit fanatical surface repair. Other times, a near-perfect job is the goal.

SAND WOODWORK (INTERIOR)

NEW WOOD

Often, before new wood trim is primed or stained it is rough sanded, with the grain, with 180 grit paper to remove the sharp edges found on new casings, moldings, door panels, etc. This is known as "easing the edges."

Following the priming and repair of new wood, all surfaces should be carefully sanded with #120 to #180 grit paper to remove all fuzz, excess spackle and Fix-all, and other imperfections. Sand with the grain of the wood. Although there are exceptions, hand sanding is almost always used. Machine sanding with finish sanders is impractical, and can actually damage the wood by leaving swirl patterns in the surface, and defacements where the sander plate strikes an adjacent surface while running at high speed.

Change hand-sanding paper frequently so that the paper is always "cutting" the surface with maximum effect. Be sure to finish setting any nails the carpenters may have missed. The wood should feel smooth following the sanding. Then dust carefully with a duster and vacuum around the bottom of door casings and baseboards before applying finish paint.

Special care must be taken to avoid scratching any metal hardware, such as hinges, striker plates, and locksets, and any window glass surface. The slightest touch of sandpaper to these surfaces WILL scratch them - EVERY TIME. The damage caused usually cannot be repaired.

PREVIOUSLY PAINTED WOOD

All previously painted wood trim should be washed and sanded prior to painting. This not only assures new paint adhesion, but provides an opportunity to sand out old drips, ridges, or other imperfections. Carry 180 grit paper for all surfaces and 80 grit to sand down blatant imperfections.

Again, dusting and vacuuming are called for before painting begins. Dust can be blown out of cracks and corners with an air tool or your own breath.

Be careful of splinters in wood while sanding. Sometimes these are long slivers, which can be very painful to remove.

Always wear a dust mask when sanding, and eye protection when sanding overhead.

Do not keep using a piece of sandpaper after its initial effectiveness is used up. The cost of sandpaper is minimal compared to the loss of manpower trying to do good work with used-up sandpaper.

When sanding previously painted wood, always sand with the grain because cross grain sanding marks can show up through finish coats of high quality enamels.

PRIMING WOODWORK (INTERIORS)

Prime coats on previously painted wood surfaces are usually unnecessary except for spot-priming any bare wood exposed by sanding and any repairs, particularly spackle, Fix-all, or putty. Caulk repairs will not "flash" through the finish paint like most repair materials, and do not need to be primed.

On new wood, the prime coat should be applied as if it were a finish coat. Care should be taken not to have overlaps on corners or joints as these can show through finish coats.

Always try to keep fresh air flowing through any room in which oil base primers and paints are used. In some situations (at night with no screens on doors and windows, or daytime in areas with high bug counts and no screens) it is necessary to work under poorly ventilated conditions. In this case wear an approved respirator.

Occasionally, knots in the wood will bleed through and discolor the finish coats. These knots should be shellacked before painting. Remember that the solvent for shellac is alcohol, not paint thinner.

On certain jobs, a white-pigmented lacquer wood undercoater will be sprayed on instead of enamel undercoater. This material is usually applied in two or three coats to achieve maximum build. Lacquer undercoater dries in about ten minutes, depending on air temperature and humidity, and can be sanded within an hour or two after application, but it is best to wait overnight for the product to harden sufficiently for good sanding results. The advantage of this product is that it dries rapidly, and can be built up with two or three coats to a very solid opaque finish in a very short period of time. The disadvantage is that adjacent surfaces must be protected from overspray.

REPAIR WALLS AND CEILINGS

Walls and ceilings come in a wide variety of conditions. The object of their preparation is to make the finished product look good and to ensure it lasts as long as possible. Preparation of each surface will vary from job to job, the extent to be determined by the job supervisor, on site, in line with the number of hours allocated in the estimate. Each situation requires specific knowledge of the surface condition and the best remedial techniques applicable. It is imperative to know what is expected and to proceed accordingly.

Prior to preparing walls and ceilings, be sure that all floors and furniture are covered with plastic or dropcloths and that access to all surfaces is assured. MOVE FURNITURE CAREFULLY! Many antique items are not as strong as you are. Breakable objects should be taken out of the room.

Use two-mil plastic from twelve foot wide rolls to cover furniture. Tape on the bottom underside of furniture to hold loose flaps. Use canvas dropcloths on floors and rugs. Sometimes six-mil plastic is taped onto a nice floor to guarantee that paint spills do not penetrate. Do not leave tape on floors for more than three days as it gets difficult to remove the longer it is down. Use light adhesive blue tape.

PLASTER AND LATHE

Open cracks with a putty knife or crack opener. Try to dig back behind the crack to create a wedge to hold the filling material in. Fill holes and cracks that are too large for spackle with Fix-All, pushing deep into the crack to lock it in as it expands and dries. Wipe with a wet sponge after fifteen minutes (before Fix-All is fully hardened) to remove excess residue.

Texture with the appropriate material: spackle, joint compound, heavy body paint, etc. Caulk corners if needed. Some cracks should be caulked because of their tendency to move or shift. Hairline cracks can often be filled with a heavy body paint. Sometimes it is advisable to use fiberglass tape and elastomeric filler or joint compound on active cracks.

Often, old plaster ceilings exhibit sufficient deterioration that they should be torn down and replaced. Occasionally, we'll roll on two coats of VIP-type elastomeric sealer to try to hold a bad ceiling together for as long as possible.

Do not remove light fixtures if it can be avoided. Old wiring is not the best place to learn how to be an electrician.

SHEETROCK

Open cracks and cut out loose sheetrock paper. Sometimes there are bubbles under the paper that must be cut out with a razor blade. You can fill deep cracks and holes with Fix-All, again remembering to sponge off residue before it dries completely and gets too hard to easily remove. Texture to match the existing surface with the appropriate material, which could be joint compound or Plaster of Paris.

Caulk door casings, baseboards, crown moldings, and window frames as needed. Always keep a wet rag with you while caulking to keep your smoothing finger clean.

Following completion of these repairs it is best to prime the new work with an appropriate product, and clean up as much debris as possible from the floor and adjoining surfaces.

PLASTER COVERED WITH CANVAS

In many older homes the plaster walls and ceilings were covered with canvas material prior to painting. This maintains a uniform look on all surfaces in spite of hairline cracks in the plaster. Large cracks will show up, however, by bubbling or stretching the canvas. Depending on the condition of the canvas it can either be completely removed from the plaster, partially removed from the plaster around the repair, or, using a razor blade, cut and folded back from the repair so that it can be pasted down after the repair is completed.

Usually it is best to leave as much of the canvas covered surface intact as possible. Occasionally, old paint will develop a crackled condition on the canvas, in which case all of the canvas must be removed and the un-derlying plaster prepared for paint.

TONGUE AND GROOVE WOOD

Frequently, it is desirable to refinish or paint out natural wood walls and ceilings. If they have been previously coated with a gloss varnish or enamel they should be washed and sanded to ensure adhesion of new finishes. When painting is desired, the prime coat usually must be applied and dried before repair work is attempted. Only then can the extent of the necessary repairs be assessed. As usual, judgment is called into play here. Sometimes, extensive caulking and filling will be required. Other times the surface will be acceptable as is.

SHEETROCK OR PLASTER COVERED WITH WALLPAPER

There are many and varied circumstances relating to the problem of preparing a wallpapered wall for paint. Due to the uncertainty involved in these projects, they are often bid on a time and materials basis. Generally speaking, it is best to remove all wallpaper and paste from a wall or ceiling before painting. (See Wallpaper Removal section). However, many situations dictate alternate procedures. Often you will find multiple layers of wallpaper, or wallpaper that has been painted over or even textured over.

If you do not want to go to the expense of removal, prime the wallpaper with an oil base primer to seal the surface, repair as needed, and re-prime the repairs. Sometimes two coats of primer is a good idea, particularly if a latex top coat is to be used (or a lot of joint compound is used) because the wetness will bubble unsealed wallpaper from the wall. If possible, use an oil base paint for the finish coat.

CONCRETE, BRICK, AND STUCCO

These surfaces should be free from dust and dirt, and all loose paint or mortar should be scraped off. Use a masonry conditioner as a primer. Be sure any efflorescence is removed. Often, a block filler (heavy body paint) is used to even out the surface appearance prior to application of the finish coats. When the surface goes below an exterior water line and is subject to moisture penetration, a special water-repellent primer is used. Some interior stucco surfaces need repairs such as those described under Plaster and Lathe.

WALLPAPER REMOVAL

Some wallpaper will peel right off, leaving only a paper backing or paste. It should all be removed completely from the surface to be painted.

Wallpaper, paper backing, and paste are best removed by soaking the paper with a soapy water solution (applied by Hudson sprayer, brush, or roller) until it is wet enough to come off easily with a wallpaper scraper. This usually involves many repeat soakings. If the paper does not come off easily, it is not wet enough.

Care must be exercised not to damage the underlying wall with the scraper, as this only adds to the amount of preparation needed after the removal process. Using hot water and a sponge or scotch-brite pad, wipe the walls clean of all paste residue while it is still wet from the removal.

Sometimes foil-type or vinyl papers will need to be scratched to allow the water to penetrate. This should be done with #36 sandpaper and a power sander or special etching tools like the Paper Tiger. This technique is also effective on paper that has been primed or painted previously.

Occasionally you will encounter a situation where the wallpaper was hung directly on untreated sheetrock. This means the sheetrock paper also gets soaked and ruined during the removal process and the walls must then be fully primed and re-textured completely. It is best to try to paint over this wallpaper without removing it, if possible.

Always protect floors from excess water and wet paper. Do not track messy, wet paper into other rooms.

Be careful around electrical outlets, switches, and light fixtures. Water will short them out.

Keep the wet paper in large plastic garbage bags and remove to the proper trash disposal area.

RAZOR WINDOW GLASS

There are many situations where razoring old paint from window glass is desirable. First of all, the new work will look better with old paint removed. Second, by razoring the edge of the glass all around, the new paint that is applied can seal the surface more effectively.

Razor blade holders are often used for this kind of work. Because of the short work life of most razor holders, some painters prefer to simply use the single edge blade held in their hand.

Razor blades are very dangerous and must be stored, used, and disposed of carefully. Never keep razor blades with other tools. Exercise extreme caution when using, and dispose of separately from other trash, protected so that no one accidently sticks their hand into something and gets cut.

Never leave razor blades lying around (used or unused). Children are attracted to them and can quickly and seriously injure themselves.

New windows and multi-pane doors often have excess putty or caulk that must be carefully razored off prior to applying any paint or primer. Sometimes, this can be very time consuming. Glass can scratch very easily, and is costly to replace. Be careful.

When the glass has been back-glazed with caulk, as is often the case with new work, conform the razor cut with the wood, and it will look clean and sharp.

Razor blades will lose their sharp edge very quickly doing this kind of work. Do not hesitate to use new blades as soon as both edges of the old blade are dull. A new blade is much easier and safer to use. Work proceeds faster and looks better.

WASHING WINDOWS

It is often advisable to clean windows before applying the final coat of paint. Clean windows can provide a definite psychological advantage during the last stages of a job. Often following a maximum paint job, filthy windows will make a room look just as dingy as it did when you started. It is worth an extra hour to correct this.

Unfortunately, many people do not know how to clean windows, and because they think it is unimportant, all they will do is spread the dirt around and make the window look streaked and not much better than before. If you're going to do it, do it right.

Use a product like Windex with newspaper (crumpled up) or clean rags or paper towels to clean the glass. Repeat as needed. Keep a new razor blade handy to get accumulated grime out of corners, and to razor off old paint specks.

Professional window cleaners often use a soft brush in a light cleaning solution and soak the whole window then use a squeegee and a dry towel to finish it off.

When re-doing exteriors, one often has to replace window putty. In this situation, it is important that you clean the window because the new putty will stay soft under the new paint for many weeks. If someone comes in to wash the window after you, they will not be aware of the soft putty and can easily disfigure it or break the paint seal on the glass.

PAINTING INTERIOR WOODWORK AND DOORS

Following full preparation, painting of interior woodwork begins. Generally, it is most efficient to paint the crown molding first, followed by windows, and trim, then door casings, and then the doors themselves. Baseboards are done last, usually after the walls have been finished.

After the ceiling itself has been painted, the crown molding will be painted. It is important to keep a wet edge while painting crown molding (and other woodwork), as lap marks will be very visible.

Preparing the Paint

Paint must be clean (strain through a filter if needed) and thinned to the proper consistency. Thinning oil paint properly is a very important aspect of the painting process. Not too little, and not too much. The paint should be thin enough to allow for smooth brushing, i.e. no "dragging or pulling", and yet not so thin that it lessens its ability to provide good color coverage. It is better to start out using too little thinner, and add more if needed, than to over-thin.

Brush Technique

With the gradual decline of alkyd oil base paints available for purchase, and their replacement by acrylics (latex), brushing technique becomes more critical. It takes many years to develop true craftsmanship with a brush. Paint must be "laid off" when brushed on so that there are no bristle marks or signs of overlapping paint, not to mention sags, drips, runs, dirt in the paint, etc. A painter's brush technique will always be improving. After fifteen years of painting, the true craftsman will recognize an improvement over the previous five years.

The objective of excellent brushwork is to make the surface to which paint is being applied look as flawless as humanly possible. In many cases, spray equipment is used to achieve this effect but often spray set-ups are not practical and brush technique is required.

There are many factors and nuances involved with custom brushwork.

Among them are the importance of straight cut-in lines; the ability to concentrate on the job sufficiently to avoid "holidays" or light areas in the enamel; avoidance of unsightly overlaps; elimination of corner paint build-ups; ability to load the brush with paint properly, and to get the paint from the bucket to the painting surface as rapidly and smoothly as possible. Other important considerations include full awareness of every drip and spatter to come off of your brush, or out of your pail, with immediate clean-up where necessary; knowledge of proper baseboard brushing technique; ability to keep paint clean while working, free of dust and debris; attunement to paint drying conditions and how quickly touch-up can be accomplished successfully, and so on.

There is no substitute for years of experience because conditions vary from day to day, and hour to hour.

Use two-gallon paint pails whenever possible. Keep the paint level in the pot high enough to dip the brush in 2 to 3 inches, but not so full that its weight makes it hard to hold up while painting. Always keep the bucket as close to your brushing hand and as near the surface being painted as you can. Do not waste effort. It is easy to work hard and get very little done. Results are what count.

Dip the brush into the paint two to three inches, bring the brush out of the paint and lightly slap the broad sides against the inside of the pail. This holds the paint on the bristles, while allowing a lot of paint to stay on the brush. Many people make the mistake of removing most of the paint that a brush will hold when they wipe it on the side of the can after loading it up with paint. The more paint on the brush, the more area covered with each brush stroke.

Begin painting woodwork one section at a time, being sure to wipe off overlaps on unpainted sections if they will not be finished before the paint begins to set-up or dry. Always unload the paint onto an unpainted area and brush back into the wet edge from the previous brush-full. Lay the paint off in the direction appropriate for that section of wood, usually with the grain.

At the bottom of door casings and baseboards and other areas where the paint work adjoins an area or surface that is not to be painted, unload the bulk of the paint from the brush well away from the cut-in edge.

Then, using a relatively dry brush, use the edges of the bristles to make the cut. This will prevent overloading and messy clean-up in these areas.

Keep moving along while painting woodwork. Always look back occasionally to make sure everything is OK. Do not stop in the middle of any section for any reason. Continue to a good breaking point before taking a coffee break or lunch.

Wood and metal frame windows require particular attention to be sure that they are properly sealed and protected by the paint. Good cut-in technique is required to adequately accomplish this task. Paint the inside sash first, and the outer casing and sill last.

A common mistake in painting multi-pane windows or doors is to miss one little section here or there. The best way to avoid this is to adopt a consistent methodical approach to these situations, and use it every time.

When cutting-in woodwork against walls and ceilings that have not been finish coated, it is usually best to cut slightly onto the wall or ceiling so that when the final cut-in is done with the wall paint it will be easier to make the straightest possible line.

A note: The straightest looking line may not be straight at all. This kind of work requires knowledge of the most effective way to make an uneven surface appear to have a straight, clean line cut on it. The painter must develop an eye for this, and know the best way to get the best looking finished product.

Doors and cabinets come in all shapes and sizes but usually can be described as smooth, single panel, or multiple panel. Often, smooth and single panel doors can be painted with a short-nap roller, and then the paint can be "laid off" with a brush, leaving the appearance of fine brush work. The advantage to this technique is that paint can be applied much more rapidly with the roller, and laying-off has to go quickly to be effective. For doors and cabinets to look their best, joints where the direction of the grain changes should be laid off properly.

When only one side of a door is being painted, be sure that any paint that rolls over an edge onto the other side is wiped off promptly. Multiple panel doors are usually painted panel by panel, with the outer edges painted last. Be careful of overlaps with multiple panel doors because sometimes paint sets up too fast to get back to it in time to be brushed out, and can leave unsightly lap marks.

When painting wood frame windows and sills, be sure that the paint does not drip onto an exterior side where it will look unsightly from the outside.

Always pick out visible pieces of debris that you can see while the paint is still wet and can be laid off again with the brush. Keep an eye out for individual bristles, broken tips of bristles, and bugs. Whenever possible get them out as you go. If bugs land in the paint after it has been par- tially set up, it is best to leave them there until after the paint has com- pletely dried. Then remove them as carefully as possible with a clean rag and touch up the spot with a small artist's brush.

It is important to have a well-lit work area at all times.

Occasionally, painters "mitts" or "gloves" are used to apply paint to cast iron railings, spindles, etc. Other times a "long John" roller, with a nar- row roller cover and a long thin handle, is used to get into places a brush cannot reach.

PRIME CEILINGS & WALLS (INTERIOR)

Normally in re-do situations, if two coats of finish paint are to be applied, a prime coat is unnecessary. Sometimes when the finish color is very dark, the repairs on the walls and ceiling should be primed using a color and product similar to the original. Some very deep or very light colors require a fully primed background because of their transparency.

Be certain that every square inch of floor and furniture is covered. Cleaning up roller or spray-gun overspray is time consuming and expensive. In rooms with furniture, be careful when moving ladders and tools around.

On all new sheetrock, following completion of the texture coat by the sheetrock sub-contractor, a coat of PVA sealer is applied either by brush and roller, or spray. This seals the paper topcoat of the sheetrock and all taping joints.

New plaster should similarly be fully primed, preferably with an oil primer. New plaster must be completely cured (dry) before priming.

The prime coat must be applied as if it was the finish coat on all smooth textured surfaces. Any ridges or roller marks will show through subsequent coats. Use smooth nap rollers for these jobs

On two coat latex flat wall jobs, the first coat serves as a prime coat.

In situations where only one coat of similar color is called for, repairs must be primed before painting, otherwise they will "flash" and show up on the finish coat with a different sheen (usually duller) than the surrounding area.

PAINTING CEILINGS

Most ceilings are cut-in with a brush around the edges and light fixtures, and rolled out. Some wood ceilings are brushed or sprayed.

When rolling ceilings, always be sure everything in the room is protected, and any areas that might be affected by even the slightest breeze should also be protected (i.e. exterior window sills because of open windows, or doorways into other rooms). Roller spray can also reach adjacent floors, draperies, interior sills, hardware, etc.

In order to maintain a wet edge while painting, always roll lengthwise on the narrowest section and work from one end of the room to the other. When using daylight only to illuminate the room, start rolling near the brightest window and roll away from it, looking back towards the light as you go. This will lessen the chance of holidays or light areas.

Work out of a five gallon bucket whenever practical. Use roller trays only for small jobs. Load as much paint on the roller as it will safely hold and always roll from an unpainted section back into the wet edge. Be careful not to leave "roller ridges" from excess paint on the outer edge of the roller cover.

Do not roll out ceilings from a ladder. Use an extension pole. Be careful that the other end of the pole does not scrape or gouge walls or furniture. Usually, because the walls will be done after the ceiling, the ceiling cut-in should come down slightly onto the wall. However, when cutting in a ceiling against a wall or crown molding that is not scheduled to be painted, do not let the paint come down onto that surface at all as this makes for a more distracting look than if a little edge is left unpainted on the ceiling. Err on the side of the ceiling and it will be less noticeable.

Often, minor imperfections on the surface of the ceiling can be hidden by rolling out that area with an especially heavy application of paint, using the extra roller texture to deflect light around the area, making it less noticeable. Hairline cracks can sometimes be filled and covered using this approach. Sometimes, a heavy bodied paint is used to build texture on an especially uneven surface.

Wood ceilings that have to be brushed out should be done board by board, or even section by section, always remembering to maintain a wet edge. Often two or three boards can be done at once, but that will depend on the drying conditions in the room at the time. The same applies to spraying ceilings.

When rolling, always keep the roller from going directly over your head to keep spray from getting in your eyes, face and hair. Many painters wear a hat and goggles when rolling ceilings. Some cheaper paints spray and spatter more than others. Occasionally, it is advisable to wear a long sleeved shirt and gloves because of the amount of spray from the roller. Using better quality paints will allow you to avoid this problem.

PAINTING WALLS

Most walls are painted by first doing all of the cut-in work with a brush and then rolling out the larger spaces.

The brush cut-in is very important and is a skill that develops slowly but surely through practice. It is critical when a dark wall color is cut in next to a light trim color. Certain ways of cutting in involve not so much how straight the cut-in line is, but where it is in relation to human sight lines. The line should appear to be straight even though it may not accurately conform to edge lines.

When brushing cut-in, lay out a nice, even amount of paint and allow enough width for a roller to roll easily into the area without having to get too near the woodwork and ceiling.

Taping baseboards, light switches, thermostats and other areas subject to roller spray is always a good idea. (However, some high quality paints are now formulated not to spray and spatter when used with high quality roller covers). When to tape depends on the demands of the situation at hand. Many times, multiple coats are required on the baseboard at the same time the walls are being painted. Taping is difficult under these circumstances.

Other times the baseboards are not part of the job at all. Then it is often best to do the cut-in at the base first, and tape lightly right before rolling, pulling the tape up immediately afterward to prevent it from sticking or pulling up old paint. Do not paint onto the tape, because paint will almost always creep under the tape edge.

Rolling out the walls should be the smoothest part of the job. Everything should be set-up to proceed rapidly. Always be sure to eliminate roller ridges as you go. Keep the tray or bucket that you are rolling out of near you. Roll from an unpainted area back into the wet edge. After rolling out a small section, use the somewhat dry roller to even out the transition area between the cut-in and the roller. The roller cut-in should come as close as possible to the edge of all walls, without getting on any adjoining surfaces. Again, the more time you spend with a roller in your hand the easier it becomes.

Learn to rapidly load as much paint as possible onto the roller every time. Some old-timers dip the whole cover into the paint, pull it out and give it a little twist to hold the paint on. Then, in one movement, the handle is brought to the wall and rolling begins. They get about twice the mileage out of one roller-full this way. This is not recommended for today's painters except under carefully controlled conditions. Unless someone has practiced this technique quite a bit, it can be very messy.

Another favorite technique of old-timers is to brush out all the walls and ceilings with a 6" brush. Surprisingly, some of these guys can out-perform many of today's "ace" painters, and make it look easy in the process.

The fact is that there are certain muscles and movements that develop over a period of time that make the job easier for the more experienced painter. We develop special calluses to aid us in our work in the same way that a concert pianist or a ditch digger develops themselves physically to keep practicing their particular skills. This is one of the arguments for encouraging people to choose a skill and develop it to its fullest extent.

PAINTING BASEBOARDS

Baseboards are usually the last item to be painted in interior work. The cut-in involved here can make a job look sharp, or, on the other hand, ragged. Many times they are caulked during the preparation procedures so that a smooth, straight line is possible. Always vacuum with a narrow nozzle (crevice tool) before painting. Get all of the dirt and fuzz off the floor or it will be pulled up by your paint brush.

When the baseboard is on a hardwood floor, it is important that no paint roll down onto the floor. This is accomplished by using less paint on the brush to begin with, and then cutting in against the floor with a "dry" brush after most of the load has been brushed out in a less sensitive area.

Similarly, when cutting in the top of the baseboard against the walls it is best to brush slightly up on the wall, and make your straight line on that side. This is actually easier to do than cutting a line on the board side; plus, it makes the baseboard easier to clean during the life of the paint job.

Painting baseboards that abut rugs is a little trickier, depending on how thick the rug is. Sometimes, a wide (12" or more) taping knife blade is used to make a clean area for cutting in. Other times the rug must be taped down with masking tape prior to painting. This is often the best method with thick rugs. Do not rely on the tape to keep paint from soaking under it. Remove tape after the paint is dry. If there is too much paint on the tape, it can pull paint off the baseboard when it is pulled up, and ruin a good job.

CLEANING HARDWARE

What constitutes "clean" hardware is somewhat subjective. We are referring to hardware that has old paint still visible on it, or distracting amounts of dirt, dust or grease adhering to it, that detract from the look of a finished paint job.

Chrome hardware can often be cleaned with "fine" steel wool or just a clean rag. Old paint can be removed with paint remover, or coarser steel wool. Sometimes there is so little old paint, just around the edge, that it can be quickly scraped off with a putty knife, being careful not to scratch the chrome, then polished with steel wool.

Brass hardware is cleaned in much the same way. Although old brass hardware can often be polished to its original sheen, this is not our definition of "clean." Discretion is important here. The objective is to make the hardware look good on the paint job. Some people will send the hardware out for the full re-plating treatment at a specialty metal shop. This is fine, but not usually necessary.

Sometimes, chrome plates or other metal types of hardware are too far gone to be easily cleaned up. In this case it is best to replace or just paint them.

Plastic switch plate covers can be cleaned by soaking in TSP for a few minutes and then rinsing off. Previously painted plastic switch plate covers can be soaked in a thick TSP solution for an hour or so and then rinsed clean. Magnetic latch mechanisms can also be cleaned this way.

REPLACING HARDWARE

It is best to organize all of the hardware and screws before replacing them so that you are certain that all the screws are with the correct pieces of hardware.

When replacing door and window latch hardware, be sure that everything works properly before moving on to the next piece. Many times some slight adjustment is needed to get a window to latch properly, or a door to close tight.

Tighten all screws firmly, but do not force them. Be careful not to strip screw heads or scratch the hardware with your screwdriver.

Extreme care must be exercised not to scratch or mar the adjoining newly painted surfaces while replacing hardware. To have to do touch-up painting at this point can be difficult and expensive "make work" that you're not getting paid for.

In many cases, in old homes particularly, various screws and sometimes pieces of hardware are missing. Try to place screws in such a way that the missing ones will not be readily noticed. Special trips to hardware stores or salvage yards to find these screws or pieces is another option, although these are time consuming and therefore expensive trips.

EXTERIOR

PROCEDURES

EXTERIOR WASHING

Previously painted exterior surfaces must be cleaned thoroughly prior to painting. This assures that the new paint will adhere properly to the old paint. This is especially critical on surfaces that have been painted with gloss enamels. Those surfaces are often sanded following washing to ensure adequate bonding between coats of paint. Often, proper washing is the most important part of the job.

There are many approaches and attitudes with regard to the importance of exterior washing. Some painters will never wash; some will rinse the building off with a hose; many advocate a high pressure water wash; a few will use scrub brushes and a hose, and will scrub and rinse every square foot of an exterior before proceeding with repairs and painting. This last method is generally the best. Some situations may not require that degree of thoroughness, however.

Always start at the top and work down. First rinse an area with the hose, then dip your scrub brush into a 1/2 full five gallon bucket of TSP and water, then scrub a small section and dip again. Proceed methodically so that nothing is missed. Carry a smaller brush to get into corners and tight areas, and to do windows and trim. Rinse with the hose while the TSP wash is still wet. Rinse off plants and bushes as you go. Sometimes it is advisable to use a clean sponge or scotch-brite pad during the rinsing process to ensure the removal of all residual TSP and dirt.

Caution! Don't ever direct intense spray at windows or around doors or up into the rafters because very often the water will leak into the house and cause walls, ceilings, or woodwork to water stain. Always use the mist setting on your nozzle when rinsing around these areas.

While washing have someone check interior windows and doors for water penetration so you have a chance to clean up any water before it has a chance to stain an interior surface.

Get to know the house, and plot out your job and all the ladder sets you'll need during the washing process.

Mildew that remains after the TSP wash can be neutralized with a solution of 1/2 bleach, 1/2 water, brushed or wiped on, prior to painting.

SCRAPE LOOSE PAINT

It is essential that all loose paint is removed from all surfaces prior to painting. There are many approaches to this task. Generally we advocate the scraper-in-hand technique. In other words, go over every inch of walls and woodwork with a keen eye and a ready hand. However, it is not always so simple.

There are several contending forces surrounding the extent of "maintenance" painting necessary and the degree of "beautification", "restoration" or simply "cosmetic" changes involved, versus the amount of money or time one is willing, or able, to spend.

In some cases, high pressure water systems are used to remove loose paint. These machines must be operated by an experienced technician. Constant attention must be directed towards cleaning up interior leaking around windows, doors, and rafters before it stains the interior surface. High pressure water can break windows, and ruin nearby plants and shrubs. The same problems exist with sandblasting.

Occasionally there are situations where complete removal of paint is called for. Methods include: brushing on chemical removers and scraping as the paint softens; using a high powered heat gun to soften the paint prior to scraping, or using a propane torch flame to soften the paint (usually the most expedient method). Always have a hose set-up and a fire extinguisher available when using any of these methods.

When scraping with a 2" flexible blade putty knife, or any other kind of scraper, be careful not to unnecessarily gouge or mar the underlying surface from which you are scraping the loose paint. Be sure, however, to scrape all loose materials out of cracks and around them.

Often, loose paint will be barely discernable on the surface and can only be detected with a practiced eye. Sometimes by tapping the paint lightly with a putty knife you can hear the slightly hollow sound of detached paint.

Similarly, little fissure cracks can lead to wide areas of loose paint that would not have been detectable without the tell-tale fissure. This loose paint may not become evident for months, or even years after a paint job, but eventually it will give way and ruin what might otherwise be an excellent job.

Check every corner and crevice for loose paint. Try to get it all the first time around. Clean up as you go. Paint particles on any cement, wood, or brick floor will grind color or scratches into the floor and become very difficult to clean off. Keep dropcloths on the ground and sweep up pieces that get on walkways. Always remember when painting, if you see some loose paint you missed, scrape it off before continuing to paint.

When there are many layers of old paint, and restoration is not the objective, but maintenance and protection is, try to feather the edge of the scraped area with your putty knife or scraper, and when priming and painting, fill the edges with paint as much as possible to even out the finished look.

Always wear a dust mask while scraping, and goggles when scraping overhead.

This work can seem tedious at times, though still enjoyable since every bit of loose paint you remove is one less problem for someone else to have to deal with. Nevertheless, it is critical to the successful completion of a professional paint job, which looks good and lasts a long time.

OLD PAINT REMOVAL

Certain situations require complete removal of old paint in order to adequately prepare a surface for new paint. Paint removal is always a dangerous and tricky procedure no matter what the method.

Sandblasting
For exterior stucco, or cement walls and floors only.

Chemical Removers
These can be brushed, rolled, or sprayed on, depending on the scope of the job. These products soften the old paint so that it can be scraped or washed off. Fumes from most chemical removers are somewhat toxic and should be applied with a respirator on. Contact with the skin or eyes can lead to hospitalization. Always wear rubber gloves and safety glasses. Always read the directions and precautions on the product label before using. Keep this material off of all other surfaces as it can cause immediate and permanent damage in many cases.

Propane Torches
Proper use of torches can be the most efficient way to soften old paint before removal with scrapers or putty knives. However, the danger of starting a fire is ever-present. It is illegal in some areas. A fire extinguisher and hose set-up must be on hand at all times.

Safety Procedures
1. Always wet down the roof and grounds adjacent to the work area.
2. Always have the hose on with the gun nozzle attached and within reach.
3. Never set a torch down while it is still burning.
4. Complete all burning operations two hours before leaving the job site.
5. At the end of each day, clean up all burned debris, and place in a fireproof container or bucket of water.

Heat Guns and Pads
These work in much the same way as a torch, and present many of the same dangers, but are much slower to use.

REPAIRING EXTERIOR CRACKS AND GAPS

Minor Stucco Repairs

Generally speaking, a material that is flexible (elastomeric) when dry is best to use on a stucco surface. There are many grades and types of caulks and fillers now on the market. Try to use the best product available at your local retail outlets for most repairs. Specialty products such as VIP are elastomeric and maintain substantial flexibility when dry.

Most of these materials are hard to work with once they start to set up and must be applied correctly the first time.

There are heavy body paints that can be brushed into small cracks and joints to form an effective seal.

Particularly large cracks are sometimes bridged with fiberglass tape, embedded in the appropriate elastomeric filler.

Occasionally, stucco or cement walls will have large areas of severe deterioration. These must be cleaned out, wetted to aid adhesion, and built back up with the appropriate stucco repair material. Often, heavy body paint filler is used to blend these repairs into the existing walls.

Most cracks need to be "opened up" before repairing because there usually is some loose material in or around the crack due to moisture penetration or movement. This can be accomplished with a putty knife, scraper, or crack opener (like a can opener). Small hairline cracks can sometimes be filled with paint or a sealer.

Minor Wood Repairs

To repair large defacements on wood surfaces such as wood siding, doorjambs, fascia boards, etc., a waterproof fiberglass auto body filler such as Bondo is used. This material is applied according to instructions using the catalyst provided and will set up and be ready for sanding or shaping within a few minutes. Bondo repairs should be primed prior to applying finish paint.

For smaller holes use linseed oil putty or glazing compound. Both of these products will dry as non-soluble in water.

For an effective repair on wood sills, the surface should be primed, then repaired by floating Bondo and sanding smooth, or use fiberglass tape and a product like Krack-Kote or V.I.P. (buttering grade).

Old wooden windows often develop wood splitting problems. Because this wood is actively shrinking and expanding with the cold and heat, caulk or an elastomeric filler is best for repair over a fiberglass tape base. Spackle is almost useless because it is water-soluble. Although it can make everything look fine today, as soon as a small crack opens up and moisture is able to penetrate, the appearance and protection begin to break down.

If spackle is used, it must be fully primed with an oil-base primer because latex paints will not keep moisture out sufficiently to prevent contact, and the spackle will not stand up to any amount of moisture penetration. Similar problems exist with Fix-all and other products that react to water.

Only use spackle, Fix-all, or similar products on areas that are not subject to any movement.

All exterior repairs should be primed before painting.

Caulking

Caulking around windows and doors is always recommended if there are any cracks or gaps. Any place on wood walls that permits water to get behind the paint should be caulked for maintenance purposes. In many cases, gaps in wood siding are caulked wherever there is a need for a better visual appearance. To be effective, caulk must be driven under pressure, deep into the crack.

SANDING EXTERIOR WOODWORK

Although in many cases, the TSP wash of exterior window and door trim is sufficient to provide for a paintable surface, on glossy surfaces, sanding prior to painting is required.

Sanding does not take the place of cleaning under any circumstances. However, it complements cleaning and really ensures that the new paint product will stick to the old. Always use the correct "grit" of sandpaper for the job at hand. Often it is wise to carry a few choices with you.

Do not over-use a piece of sandpaper. When it's not cutting with efficiency, get a new piece.

Sanding is also useful to smooth out or "feather" rough looking edges resulting from scraping loose paint. The older the house (i.e. the more layers of paint) the harder it is to "feather." More time is always spent detailing high traffic areas (those most frequently seen) leading to front doors or around decks, etc. than is spent on 3rd floor window sills or casings.

Complete restoration of a surface occurs when it is scraped or sanded to bare wood, primed, and painted. Unless this approach is specified, it is not to be sought after as it results in two to three times the work, and may not be appropriate for the job.

Most exterior sanding can be done by hand. Sometimes a power sander such as an orbital or disc sander is used. These tools should be used by experienced personnel only. Improper use will result in "chattering" or disc grooves in the old paint which can be more unsightly than the original surface and harder to repair later.

Many paints do not sand well, and should not be continuously sanded in one spot with an electric sander because it will cause the paint to heat up and bubble or become gummy.

All bare wood should be primed before painting.

OPENING STUCK WINDOWS

Be careful not to break windowpanes while attempting to open a stuck window. Some windows are nailed shut. Some are painted shut. Start with the painter's window opener, a saw-like tool that is shaped to saw into the dried paint where it's holding the window. Go all around the framed areas. Loosen the moving parts gradually with a putty knife or pry bar. Do not damage adjacent wood surfaces.

Windows that are stuck because of new paint will open easily once the sticking point is ascertained. They may need to be touched up after they are opened. The longer drying time allowed, the better. Many people do not like their windows open at night, these should be painted early in the morning so they'll be dry later in the day. Always close them carefully. Try to avoid sticking.

Sometimes it's good to move windows slightly while they are drying to keep them from sticking. Once is usually enough. It will depend on the skill of the painter to minimize these effects.

Often, windows are meant to be sealed shut for security reasons.

Some old windows should not be tampered with unless replacement is the objective. Because of rotten or broken wood they can be very dangerous.

REPLACING LOOSE WINDOW PUTTY

The maintenance objective of exterior window painting is to seal and protect all surfaces from moisture penetration and preserve the window so it
doesn't have to be replaced, which is usually an expensive proposition,
especially in older homes and buildings. To achieve this, you should remove all loose window putty and re-glaze as needed.

Technically speaking, if there is any loose putty, the whole line section of
putty, from corner to corner, should be removed. Our position usually
is... if we have to chisel it out, it's not loose.

Always be careful when removing loose putty. Professional glaziers
make special knives that they use by lightly tapping with a hammer. We
often use our putty knife or scraper, and occasionally a chisel. It is very
easy to crack a pane of glass when removing putty or cleaning residue.
It is also quite a bit more expensive to replace the cracked glass. Use
caution. Corners are particularly susceptible to cracking under light
pressure.

Remembering that a good seal is the objective, the new putty must adhere to a clean, dry surface, free from dust and debris. Bare wood and
rusted metal should be primed first before puttying.

Press the putty firmly into the area being re-done, either with your fingers, palm, or putty knife. When you are sure the putty is firmly in place,
draw your putty knife, blade down, slowly, with light pressure, from one
end of the re-do to the other. Excess putty will squeeze out both sides of
the blade and can be carefully removed once you are satisfied that you
have a good looking repair that conforms to the original workmanship.

Many times one will encounter putty that has cracked and/or pulled
slightly away from the glass along the edge, but is not loose at all. The
best approach to this situation is to prime the affected areas with an oil-
base primer, being sure to fill in all gaps with as much primer as possible. After the primer has dried, putty can be rubbed into all visible
crevices, including along the glass line. This surface is then repainted,
being sure the paint makes the seal over the putty and against the glass.

REPLACE BROKEN WINDOWS

Ideally, a professional window glazier will be responsible for replacing broken glass. Like many skills, this is one that benefits from experience. However, anyone might be called upon to replace a pane or two of glass.

First, the old glass must be carefully removed. Chisel or knife out all of the window putty, then remove the "points" or "steel springs" that are used to hold the glass to its surrounding wood or metal sash.

If the glass is badly cracked, it is a good idea to completely tape both sides with masking tape to hold it together while it is taken out. If it was properly back-glazed when it was originally installed, it will need to be tapped or hammered out. Back-glazing means sealing up the inside part of the window where the glass contacts the wood or metal sash.

Once the glass is out, scrape all old putty out of the window frame. If bare wood or rusted metal is exposed, prime with an appropriate primer.

Caulk is often used in place of putty for the back-glazing of new glass. Good back-glazing can significantly extend the life of an interior paint job.

Next, the points or springs are re-inserted. Important! Glass will easily fall out due to improper setting of points or springs, even when it has been correctly puttied. Make sure there are at least two points on each side of the pane of glass (minimum eight).

The most important and visible part of the job is the exterior puttying or "glazing" of the window. Putty should be kneaded prior to application to eliminate air pockets.

When the putty is the correct consistency, take a palm size ball and methodically press the putty into place, trying to squeeze it deep into the corners and firmly against the glass and wood or metal. Work the putty continuously from one ball to minimize weak points.

After the putty is roughly in place, the trimming begins. Remember, the outside putty line should not be visible on the inside. Press the putty knife into a corner and draw firmly and smoothly to the next corner. Clean off excess and continue.

The putty should set up for several days before being painted. Sometimes this is not possible. However, if it is painted too soon, or under the wrong drying conditions, the paint will crinkle on the skin of the putty. If the puttying was done properly, it will still remain tightly sealed to the glass.

When puttying is complete, use a new razor blade and a clean rag to carefully clean off the oil residue from putty on the glass. (Sometimes it's a water base putty residue)

PREPARING EXTERIOR RUSTED SURFACES

You will encounter various types of metal surfaces:

1. Galvanized Metal - cold rolled steel which is electroplated with a zinc plating. The zinc plating will not rust but will wear off and the base steel will begin rusting.

2. Ferrous Metals - those which contain iron, such as wrought iron, cast or stamped metal brackets or plates, etc.

3. Non Ferrous Metals - such as aluminum, copper, brass, or bronze. Although these metals do not rust, they will oxidize. Copper will naturally turn green over time. Uncoated aluminum will begin to pit and corrode. For this reason, many aluminum windows are anodized to prevent this condition from occurring.

Exterior rust is most often found on old galvanized metal gutters and downspouts and on iron railings. Some have deteriorated to the point where replacement is the only economical alternative. This is particularly true of galvanized metal gutters and downspouts that have rusted through from the inside out. No amount of paint is going to protect that condition, or hide it for long.

The best procedure for removing rust is to sand or sandblast the surface down to "white metal" free of all visible rust. As this is seldom practical, remove rust scale as well as possible using a wire brush or sandpaper. Then apply one coat of zinc chromate or other metal primer.

Never apply latex finish paint over a rusted surface that has been cleaned but not primed.

Whenever possible, seek to find the source of the rust or rust stain (when water has flowed over a rusted area and left a discolored streak away from it). Scrape the area clean, sand through the rust to bare metal, and prime with a specially formulated rust retardant primer. If needed, caulk any crack or crevice that might allow water to penetrate to the metal.

Follow these procedures with two coats of finish paint (preferably oil) and the job will provide many years of serviceable protection.

In the case of painted surfaces that have been streaked by rust, it is important that the cause of these streaks be found and remedied before they are painted over and forgotten about. If the cause is not eliminated, the streaks will reappear shortly after the first rainstorm. These streaks can occur in many locations and be related to roofing materials, PG&E hook-ups, interior or exterior plumbing hook-ups, antenna mounts, and so on. Sometimes caulking can eliminate this condition.

PREPARING NEW METALS

GALVANIZED METAL- New galvanized metal is usually wiped clean of manufacturing residues using a rag or sponge soaked in white vinegar. Mineral spirits can be used in place of white vinegar if needed. When dry, prime with a galvanized metal primer, tinted to match the finish coat color. Sometimes the finish coat paint itself can be used as a primer. Read the directions on the label.

FERROUS METALS - Wrought iron, cast iron, stamped metal brackets, etc. contain iron. They should be cleaned of fingerprints, grease, etc. and primed with a zinc chromate primer or other rust retardant material.

NON-FERROUS METALS - Commonly occurring are aluminum, copper, brass, and bronze. Often they are left unpainted, but not always. Each requires a particular primer to assure maximum adhesion of finish coats. As always, they must be clean before priming. Be sure you are using the correct primer.

Proper cleaning and priming of new metals can extend the life of a paint job significantly, and guarantee a good foundation for subsequent coats of paint many years down the line. Conversely, poorly prepared metal surfaces invariably are the first thing to exhibit peeling paint and often are situated in highly visible locations.

PAINTING EXTERIORS

Generally, it is best to start from the top and work down, tackling one side at a time. Circumstances will provide exceptions to this rule frequently, however. One obvious instance occurs when an exterior wall is cut in along the bottom of the wall first, so that by the time everything else is cut in, the base is dry, and dropcloths can be laid right up against the wall to protect from overspray.

Sometimes it is best to do window casings before the work is cut in; other times the reverse is true. All production sequences are determined by the circumstances at hand.

Plants, trees, walkways, roofs, and decks must be protected from roller and spray gun over-spray, and brush spatter. They can usually be covered with light dropcloths or plastic. Do not leave plastic on plants in the sunlight as the intense greenhouse effect can quickly damage them.

Some situations are suitable to use ladder jacks on a pair of extension ladders with a plank between ladders as a work platform. These take two experienced men to safely and efficiently set up and move. Any complex rigging or scaffold erection should be done under the supervision of a professional.

Scaffolding and ladder safety is an important consideration in exterior painting. The feet of the ladder should always be firmly set on a solid surface. Sometimes ladders need to be tied in place to ensure safety.

Proceed methodically, using most of the same techniques described in interior painting. Use paint to seal up and protect the exterior surfaces. Southern exposure windows, doors, and fascia boards require the most attention.

Do not paint in direct sunlight when it is hot, or when there is a threat of rain, or when temperatures are below 45-50 F.

FENCES AND DECKS

Fences and decks will require varying degrees of preparation depending on their condition and the painter's intent.

Basically they should be clean and dry, with any loose paint removed.

Decks pose special problems, particularly if the wood has started to split from exposure to the elements.

Painted decks that are exposed to rain and sun (or fog and sun) are particularly hard to maintain, and often must be re-done frequently.

It is better to stain a new deck under these conditions, using a specially formulated decking stain. Stain manufacturers recommend waiting six months for the wood to cure before painting or staining.

Sometimes the undersides of decks are treated, sometimes not, depending on the aforementioned circumstances and conditions.

Fences and decks can be brushed, rolled, or sprayed with a variety of spray units, depending on the feasibility of each approach.

Weak floor boards on a deck should be replaced. Deterioration should not be covered up or hidden by surface repairs. This creates a dangerous situation because it looks safe when it is not.

Some unpainted wood decks that have turned grey from aging may be restored to a newer looking condition by applying a product like Dekswood. Apply Dekswood according to manufacturer's instructions.

POWER TOOLS

AIRLESS SPRAY EQUIPMENT

Airless spray equipment is a marvelous time-saving invention, but as with any tool, it has limitations. The primary drawback to any spray method of paint application, either conventional air or airless, is paint overspray.

Airless spray equipment is to be used only when the net time saved by using the tool is significantly offset by the time spent in masking adjacent surfaces, covering furniture and plants, set-up and clean-up time, and all the other tasks involved when spray-painting is used. Unless this time saved really amounts to something, it is better to use hand tools to do the job than run all the risks and hassles of spraying. So, the bottom line is: Do not spray unless it is really worth it.

Advantages of spray painting:

1. Rapid paint application.

2. Uniform layoff of materials, free of brush marks and roller texture.

3. Coverage in one coat over many surfaces.

Disadvantages of spray painting:

1. Additional time spent setting up and cleaning up equipment. This includes extension cords, spray shields, respirators, fans, etc.

2. Additional time spent covering surfaces with plastic and dropcloths, and masking adjacent surfaces. Most of this would not have to be done if hand tools were used.

3. Requires a skilled operator. Because of the constant concern for overspray, only those persons who are completely alert and vigilant at all times can be allowed to use a spray gun.

The painter who is not paying attention to wind speed and direction, and to other objects in his immediate vicinity, will see the overspray after the damage is done.

Sometimes it may take hours to clean up overspray, and sometimes the over-sprayed surface simply cannot be restored no matter how much time and money is spent. Over-spray is the result of carelessness, not "an accident."

STAIN AND LACQUER TECHNIQUE

Surfaces which are to be stained and lacquered are usually cabinets and vanities (also called casework), and may include doors, door casings, bookcases, paneling, etc. Careful step-by-step work is the way to an excellent finished product. The procedures listed below are for staining and lacquering oak wood.

STEP-BY-STEP SURFACE PREPARATION

1. Make sure the work area is adequately illuminated with work lights. Sand all surfaces to remove pencil marks, sharp edges, rough surfaces, etc. 100 grit sandpaper is usually the best. Make sure all of the wood has been sanded. Take great care to avoid scratching any hardware such as brass hinges or other surfaces like glass lights. Scratched glass cannot be repaired - only replaced at a high cost. It may be desirable to mask off some glass lights before sanding work begins. After sanding is complete, blow off all surfaces with compressed air.

2. Some cabinets have a melamine or other type of laminate interior (usually white in color) and this must be protected from stain splatters and lacquer over-spray. These surfaces must be masked off completely with masking paper. Taped edges must be pressed down tight to avoid stain "bleeding" under the tape. NOTE: Masking tape is a pressure-sensitive tape. This means that the adhesive on the tape is affected by how much pressure is applied to the surface of the tape. The more pressure, the better the seal against stain "bleed." Other areas to be masked include adjacent wall surfaces.

Lacquer, although clear in color, cannot be allowed to spray onto walls even if they are to be painted or wallpapered later. The glossy lacquer will cause wallpaper to not adhere, and painted surfaces to appear non-uniform. Be certain that masking paper is "tacked" well, to avoid having un-taped edges flap back into the wet lacquer as the cabinets are being sprayed.

Before actually staining, check over the surface one last time by sight and touch to locate areas missed in the initial sanding phase. Apply oil-based wiping stain with either a 4" or 3" bristle brush. Use a good quality tool. Flood stain on and brush out uniformly so that absolutely no spots are missed.

Try to "dry brush" areas next to taped edges to avoid leaving excess stain bleed under the tape.

Sanding scratches sometimes become more visible when the stain is applied. They can, and must, be sanded out right through the wet stain with regular 100 grit paper. Sand with the grain of the wood until the scratch disappears. After a section of cabinets have been stained, they can be wiped off with folded paper towels or rags to produce a uniform surface. Do not allow stain to set-up too long or it will become tacky.

Be sure that all used paper towels or rags are placed in a five gallon bucket of water to prevent spontaneous combustion. Also, buff all hinges free of stain while it is still wet. Dried stain is difficult to remove. Stained cabinets should be allowed to dry overnight before applying sanding sealer.

LACQUER SANDING-SEALER

Hi-solids lacquer sanding sealer is sprayed on the wood to act as a lacquer primer. This prevents the finish lacquer from soaking into the wood coat after coat, and losing its gloss. If applied by conventional air spray (two gallon twin regulated pressure pot system) normal sanding sealer material reduction is one part sanding sealer to 1/2 part lacquer thinner. Make sure the sanding sealer is stirred well and is completely in solution. New, unopened containers will usually stir up well, but material that was reduced to shooting consistency and re-packaged may not stir up - and will have to be discarded. It is usually not necessary to strain the product before shooting.

PRESSURE POT SETTINGS

— approximately 50 - 70 PSI in line pressure to pot
— 40 PSI air pressure to gun
— Approximately 5 to 10 PSI fluid pressure to gun

Sanding sealer is usually applied with two full coats on all surfaces, except for the faces of cabinet doors, and detailed sculptured molding, which may require three coats. Sanding sealer is also available in a water-white grade, which is to be used over white-wash and light colored stains to avoid ambering.

RE-SANDING ALL SURFACES

Although sanding sealer dries to the touch in a few minutes and can be sanded out and lacquered within an hour or two, it is usually best to let the product dry overnight. This makes for much easier sanding the next day, as the sandpaper will cut freely and not "load up." Sand all surfaces with either 180 or 220 grit paper. 180 grit is best for broad, flat surfaces. Steel wool (usually #2 grit) is to be used on sculptured moldings and re-cessed panels, etc.

NOTE: Caution must be used to avoid "burning the edges." This means putting too much pressure on the sandpaper and sanding through the thin film of sanding sealer, and actually sanding through the stain as well, revealing the bare wood. This usually happens on outside edges of raised panel, moldings, etc. This is why "easing the edges" or removing this sharp corner is important in the initial sanding operation.

After all surfaces have been sanded and steel-wooled, blow off the dust with compressed air - usually at about 100 PSI.

FILLING NAIL HOLES

Nail holes are to be filled with color putty custom matched to the wood. This is done after the sanding sealer is sanded and surfaces dusted off and before the application of finish lacquer. This is the time to touch up any burned edges with stain to restore color. This is done by taking a small amount of stain on a clean rag and wiping over the surface. Wipe off all excess stain.

An ideal lacquer procedure would be:
Day #1 - Sand and stain
Day #2 - Apply sanding sealer
Day #3 - Sand out and fill holes
Day #4 - Apply finish lacquer

APPLICATION OF LACQUER

Lacquer is available in the following range of lusters: Flat, eggshell (also called rubbed-effect) semi-gloss and full gloss. A water-white lacquer must be used over white-washed wood. Normal reduction is 1 part lacquer to 3/4 parts lacquer thinner. Two coats is usually sufficient for most surfaces, but three and sometimes four coats may be required on some areas.

NOTE: When spraying lacquer sanding sealer and lacquer the room must be well lit and well ventilated. A large fan must be in the room at the window or door and cross ventilation must be created. Double-filter respirators and/or ambient air breathing apparatus must be worn at all times while spraying.

Check your local Air Resources Board to find out what kind of spraying is allowed in your area.

POWER TOOLS AND EQUIPMENT

PRESSURE WASHERS

Most surfaces that require cleaning can best be cleaned by the simple manual methods covered elsewhere in the procedures section. Certain surfaces, however, may require the force of high-pressure water, or the large water volume that is produced by gasoline-driven pressure washers or water blasters. An example of this kind of surface would be a painted brick wall where the mortar is crumbling, the paint is peeling, and there is evidence of efflorescence. High pressure will blast-clean this unsound surface more effectively than mechanical means. Another example would be a surface where paint removing chemicals have been applied to intricate molding detail, and the high pressure and water volume are needed to rinse the surface clean.

Water blasters must be used with caution. Depending on the machine, pressures will vary from 2,000 psi to 10,000 psi and higher. A few things to consider:

1. Water being driven under high pressure can penetrate into the interior of a building through cracks and gaps in the doors and windows and can cause expensive waterstain damage to draperies, curtains, carpets, and hardwood floors. Keep the blasting tip away from these gaps, and always have someone checking inside the building as the work progresses. Prevent damage instead of discovering it later.

2. The force of the water can destroy delicate plantings, or deface the surface of soft woods. Also, high pressure lines and water hoses being carelessly dragged around will knock over plants, break flower pots, etc. In short: Water blasting is noisy and messy. The property damage that can result may dictate that simpler cleaning methods be used. Use good judgment.

When using a water blaster:

1. Always place the machine on a level surface for two reasons: first, the machine's vibrations will cause it to "walk" down an incline, and sec-

ondly, small air-cooled gasoline engines do not have oil pumps to lubri-
cate the crankshaft bearings, so an engine slightly low on oil, set on an
incline, can become starved for oil and burn up.

2. Always use water supply hoses that are three quarters of an inch in
diameter or larger. Attach to a water supply with the maximum water
pressure and delivery.

3. Make sure that the water supply hose and the high pressure hose are
free of kinks and tight turns or loops.

4. Never add gasoline to the fuel tank while the engine is running. Keep
the gasoline can capped, and away from the machine.

5. Do not leave the machine unattended, such as on the other side of a
building. Coil the lines and hoses, and replace in the truck or van as
soon as the water-blasting portion of the work is completed. Do not
leave equipment lying around.

ELECTRIC SANDERS

There are three types of electric sanders used in the painting trade:

Orbital sanders

These sanders are referred to as finishing sanders, or, sometimes, vi-
brating sanders. These machines use either one half of a sheet of sandpaper (or in the case of palm sanders, one quarter of a sheet) and
operate at about 10,000 to 11,000 orbits per minute. They work most effectively with 50 grit and finer paper down to about 120 grit. Hand sanding is usually recommended with 150 grit and finer grades. Make sure
that the sheets of paper are divided neatly, and attached firmly without
flapping when the machine is turned on.

Change the paper as soon as it is no longer "cutting" effectively. Don't
wait to replace until the paper is completely smooth and worn out. To
protect the sander pad, remove any sheet of paper at once that has become torn by an exposed nail head or overuse. These sanders are very
safe to use, and do not require eye protection except for overhead work.
A dust mask or respirator is recommended.

Disc sanders

Disc sander-grinders come in wheel diameter sizes from 4 and one half inches (also called mini-grinders) to powerful 9" 15 amp tools. These machines are very effective at surface paint removal, which also makes them difficult to use without causing a great deal of damage and deface-ment to the surface. Only skilled, trained personnel should be permitted to operate a disc sander. Sanding discs range from 24 grit to 60 grit. Carborundum wheels may also be attached to the spindle to grind down metal bolts, studs, etc. Always attach wheel guards before using the grinding wheel. Wire brushes and wire wheels may also be attached.

Eye protection must always be worn. Ear protectors and respirators are also recommended. A helmet with a visor and built-in ear protection is available, and is an excellent accessory. Always make sure the trigger switch is off before plugging in any power tool.

Belt sanders

Because of their weight, belt sanders are only used on a limited basis to take off a lot of paint on a smooth surface in a hurry. Goggles and a res-pirator are required.

Electric screwdrivers

Battery powered electric screwdrivers or screw-guns may be used under certain conditions to remove or replace hinges, hardware, etc. A few words of caution, however:

1. It is very easy for an unskilled operator to deface slotted head or phillips head screws when using a regular screwdriver, let alone a power screwdriver. This will occur when too small or too large a bit is used with a particular screw (the fit should be just right) or if the operator allows the bit to "jump" out of the head of the screw as it is being tightened or un-screwed. DO NOT ALLOW THIS TO HAPPEN. If necessary, tighten all screws by hand.

2. Do not use power tools to re-attach plastic switch plates and outlet plates. No time is really saved, and using a power tool is a great way to

crack the plates.

3. Recharge the battery in the gun after each use. The charge must be maintained to avoid damage to the battery.

AFTERWORD

Many years of pleasurable comfort and enjoyment can be derived from an excellent and thorough paint job.

The old saying "Anyone can paint!" has always been true and still is. The patient painter can produce quality workmanship if each step is followed carefully and
assiduously, and can improve his or her skills every day.

It's hard to beat the sense of satisfaction one can get just by looking around and thinking How nice.

DICTIONARY

OF TERMS

ABRASIVE: A substance used for the wearing away of a surface by rubbing. Examples of abrasives: powdered pumice, rottenstone, silica, sandpaper, garnet paper, and steel wool.

ABSORB: To take something into it's pores, like wood absorbing a paint or stain.

ABUTMENT: The point or place where a support joins the item supported.

ACCELERATE: To quicken or hasten the natural progress of certain actions or events.

ACCESS DOOR: Any door which will provide access to a concealed space or equipment.

ACCORDION DOORS: Doors that fold in a manner similar to the bellows of an accordion and which are supported by rollers in an overhead track.

ACETONE: A water-white volatile solvent with an ether-like odor. Acetone is made by destructive distillation of hardwood, fermentation of butyl alcohol, and from petroleum sources. It is used extensively in making paint removers.

ACOUSTIC PAINT: Paint that absorbs or deadens sound.

ACRYLIC RESINS: Synthetic resins of excellent color and clarity used in both emulsion and solvent-based paints.

ACTIVATOR: A catalyst, curing agent or co-reactant, as for an epoxy resin.

ADHESION: Bonding strength; the attraction of a coating to the substrate, or of one coat of paint to another.

AIR DRY: To dry a coating at ordinary room or outside temperature and conditions.

AIRLESS SPRAYING: Spraying without atomizing air, using hydraulic pressure.

AISLE: A passage between rows of seats, as in a church.

ALCOHOL: A flammable solvent miscible with water. The alcohols commonly used in painting are ethyl alcohol as a shellac solvent, and methyl alcohol or wood alcohol in paint removers.

ALKALI: Caustic or basic substance which release hydroxyl ions in aqueous medium. Lye is the most common alkali.

ALKYD: A synthetic resin, made usually with phthalic anhydride, glycerol and fatty acids from vegetable oils, used in oil base paint.

ALLIGATORING: Condition of paint film in which surface is cracked and develops an appearance somewhat similar to the skin on the back of an alligator.

ALUMINUM PAINT: Mixture of finely divided aluminum particles in flake form combined with a paint vehicle.

AMBIENT TEMPERATURE: Room temperature or the temperature of the surroundings.

ANTECHAMBER: The compartment or room followed by a vestibule and part of the entry, serving as a waiting or reception area.

ANTI-CORROSIVE PAINT: Metal paint designed to inhibit corrosion. Applied directly to the metal.

APPENDAGE: Any structure appended or attached to the outer wall of a building.

APPRENTICE PAINTER: One engaged in learning the painting trade who is covered by a written agreement with an employer, association of employers or other responsible agency. Such an agreement provides for a certain number of years of reasonably continuous employment and for participation in an approved program of training in skills and related technical and general subjects.

APPURTENANCE: A structure that is attached to, or near the main structure so as to be considered a part of it.

APRON: A plain or molded piece of trim below the sill of a window.

ARBOR: A garden shelter made of lattice or trellis work.

ARCADE: A passageway with an arched roof, usually with shops on one or both sides.

ARCHITRAVE: A main beam being that part of the entablature which rests upon a column head and supports the frieze.

ARCHWAY: A hall or passageway that is spanned by an arch.

ASTRAGAL: A molding on the leading edge of a door. Usually a rubber molding extending the full height on center opening doors.

ATRIUM: An open courtyard area within the confines of a building.

ATTIC: That space immediately below the roof and above the ceiling of the top floor.

BACK PRIMED: When a coat of paint is applied to the back of woodwork and exterior siding to prevent moisture from entering the wood and causing the grain to swell, it is said to be □back primed."

BAFFLE: Any surface used for deflecting sound, usually in the form of a plate or wall.

BALCONY: A supported projection from the face of a wall usually surrounded by a railing.

BALUSTER: The supporting vase-shaped columns for a railing.

BALUSTRADE: A railing consisting of a handrail on balusters.

BANISTER: See balustrade.

BANQUETTE: An upholstered bench; placed against or built into a wall.

BASEBOARD: A trim piece of wood, rubber or tile covering the horizontal joint between floor and wall.

BAS-RELIEF (Pronounced "Bah"): A carving that protrudes slightly from the background.

BATTEN STRIP: A narrow trim piece used to cover the vertical joints between panels.

BEAM CEILING: Ceiling construction in which the beams of the ceiling are exposed to view.

BEARING WALL: A wall supporting any vertical load as well as its own weight.

BENZENE: Sometimes called ⬜Benzol." Often confused with "Benzine" due to similarity in pronunciation. Benzene is a very powerful aromatic solvent for many materials. Its use is restricted, however, due to its toxicity and also due to the fact that it is a fire hazard.

BEVELED: Any edge that has been angled other than at 90 degrees.

BINDER: The nonvolatile portion of a paint that serves to bind or cement the pigment particles together. Oils, varnishes and proteins are examples of binders. See Vehicle.

BITING: Solvent in topcoat dissolves or bites into coat below. If lacquer solvent is too biting, dried lacquer surface may be rough or provide an "orange peel" effect.

BLAST CLEANING: Cleaning with propelled abrasives.

BLEACHING: Restoring discolored or stained wood to its normal color or making it lighter by using bleaching agents.

BLEEDING STAIN: Stain which works up or "bleeds" through succeeding coats of finishing materials.

BLENDING: Mixing one color with another so the colors mix or merge gradually.

BLISTERING: Formation of bubbles on surface of paint or varnish film, generally caused by moisture behind the film.

BLOOM: Clouded appearance on a varnished surface.

BLOWTORCH: A gasoline or propane torch used in burning off paint film. Should be used only by experienced painters. It is a dangerous fire hazard when used by amateurs.

BOARD & BATTEN: A type of siding made of one foot boards with battens covering the vertical joints.

BODY: Thickness of a fluid. Other suitable words describing body are "consistency" or ⬜viscosity."

BODY COAT: Intermediate coat of paint between priming and finishing coats.
BONDING: Adhesion.

BREEZEWAY: A covered passage open at each end.

BRITTLE: Easily broken; not tough.

BRUSHABILITY: The ability or ease with which a paint can be brushed out.

BRUSH HAND: A painter whose ability lies in his skill in applying material.

BUBBLING: A term used to describe the appearance of bubbles on the surface while a coating is being applied, or after weathering.

BULKHEAD: Usually a wall or partition erected to hold back material such as dirt or concrete.

BULLNOSE: A rounded corner tile or the rounded edge of a stair tread or other architectural member.

BUTT JOINT (Wallpaper): Joint made by trimming both selvedges and butting the edges together. This technique is used mainly in specialized paper hanging work.

CAKING: Hard settling of pigment from paint.

CASING: The framing around a window or door.

CAST: Inclination of one color to look like another. For example, sulphur is yellow with a greenish □cast."

CATALYST: A substance which by its presence accelerates velocity of reaction between substances.

CAULKING: The filling of an opening or seam with a mastic material to prevent leaking.

CAULKING COMPOUND: A semidrying or slow drying plastic material used to seal joints or fill crevices around windows, chimneys, etc. Usually made in two grades; the gun type for application by use of a special gun; and the knife type for use with a putty knife.

CHAIR RAIL: A trim piece fastened to a wall to protect it against chair (seat) backs.

CHALKING: The decomposition of a paint film into a loose powder on the surface. Mild chalking, accompanied by satisfactory color retention in tinted paint, is considered a desirable characteristic. Heavy chalking that washes off to leave an unprotected surface is highly undesirable. Before recoating a heavily chalked surface, all of the chalk should be removed. This is usually accomplished by vigorous brushing.

CHECKING: The formation of short narrow cracks in the surface of a paint film. These cracks may assume many patterns, but the usual ones resemble the print of a bird's foot or small squares.

CHIMNEY COWL: A revolving metal ventilator placed over a chimney.

CLAPBOARD: Wood siding that is thin on one edge and thicker on the other; successive boards slightly overlap each other.

CLEAN SURFACE: One free of contamination, ready for paint.

CLERESTORY WINDOWS: A series of windows in a wall above the roof line, providing light and ventilation to the building.

CLOISTER: A square court surrounded by an open arcade.

CLOSE-GRAIN WOODS: Woods such as birch, maple, etc. where the fibers are fine and are held closely together are called close-grain woods.

COAGULATE: To change from a liquid into a dense mass; solidity; curdle.

COATINGS: Surface coverings; paints; barriers.

COAT OF PAINT: One layer of dry paint, resulting from a single wet application. Single layer of paint spread at one time and allowed to harden.

COBWEBBING: Premature drying which causes a spider web effect.

COFFER: A recessed panel or portion of ceiling.

COLD-CHECKING: Checking in a paint film caused by low temperature.

COLONNADE: A series of columns usually supporting an architrave.

COLOR: A property of visible phenomena in which certain impressions are formed on the retina of the eye by the light of different wavelengths. Color can be divided into three principal parts: hue, tint, and shade.

COLOR-IN-OIL: A paste formed by mixing a color pigment in linseed or other vegetable oil. Used principally for tinting.

COLOR MAN: The term applies to the individual--either the journeyman or con-tractor--who is an expert in tinting and matching colors.

COLOR PIGMENTS: Pigments such as blue, red etc. which absorb a portion of the light that falls upon them and reflect or return to the eye certain groups of light bands which enable us to recognize various colors.

COLOR RETENTION: When a paint product exposed to the elements shows no signs of changing color, it is said to have good color retention.

COMMON RAFTER: A rafter that extends past the wall to form the eaves.

CONCRETE: A hard strong building material made by mixing a cementing mate-rial (such as portland cement) and a mineral aggregate (such as sand and gravel) with sufficient water to cause the cement to set and bind the entire mass.

CONSISTENCY: The fluidity or viscosity of a liquid or paste; resistance of a product to flow.

COOL COLORS: Hues or colors in which blue predominates. The term "cool" is used because of the association with ice, water and sky.

CORBEL: A projecting bracket-like ledge made of masonry or wood to form a support.

CORNICE: The decorative or finish members projecting out from where the roof and side walls meet.

CORROSION: Decay; oxidation; deterioration due to interaction with the environment; eaten away by degrees.

COUNTERSINK: The recessing of a nail, screw or bolt below the plane of the surface.

COVE BASE: A concave baseboard of rubber, vinyl or tile.

COVERAGE: Amount of surface a given quantity of paint will cover; also, how well a paint conceals the surface being painted in one coat.

CRACKING: Splitting; disintegration of paint by breaks through film.

CRACKLE FINISH: A finish in which alligatoring is produced, allowing the undercoat to show through the cracks. Cracking is produced by rapid drying of topcoat over slow drying undercoat.

CRATERING: Formation of holes or deep depressions in paint film.

CRAWLING: Varnish defect in which poor adhesion of varnish to surface in some spots causes it to crawl or gather up into globules instead of covering the surface.

CRAZING: Minute, interlacing cracks on the surface of a finish.

CUPOLA: A small structure built on top of a roof.

CURING: Setting up; hardening.

CURING AGENT: Hardener promoter.

CURTAINING: Sagging.

CURTAIN WALL: A non-bearing wall, often of glass, built between piers or columns.

"CUT IN THE SASH": Painting the window sash. This is ordinarily done with a brush, often called a sash tool, which permits the painter to get a clean edge.

DADO: A decorative molding placed horizontally on the lower portion of a wall; a groove in woodwork.

DEAD FLAT: Having no gloss at all.

DECORATIVE PAINTING: Architectural painting; aesthetic painting.

DEEP (color): Intense or strong color with no apparent presence of black.

DEGREASER: Chemical solution compound (TSP or other) for grease removal.

DIMPLE: An impression left in wallboard when the fastener (the nail) is driven to the proper depth.

DISCOLORATION: Color change.

DOMINANT COLOR: Color that predominates, or is outstanding.

DORMER: A gabled cupola in a pitched roof, usually with a window.

DOUBLE HUNG WINDOW: A window with two moveable sash sections opening vertically.

DOVETAIL: An interlocking joint.

DOWNSPOUT: A pipe carrying rain water from the roof gutters to the ground or sewer system.

DRIERS: Compounds of certain metals that hasten the drying action of oils when added to paints or varnishes. Some driers are in dry form; others, in paste form. Most of them are solutions of metallic soaps in oils and volatile solvents. They are known as driers, oil driers, Japan driers, liquid driers and Japans. The metallic soaps most commonly used are those of lead, manganese and cobalt.

DRIFT: (Overspray) Spray loss.

DROP CEILING: A lowered ceiling.

DROP CLOTH: A large piece of fabric used by a painter while painting a room to protect furniture, rugs and other articles from paint damage.

DRY TO HANDLE: Time interval between application and ability to pick up without damage. A film of paint is "dry to handle" when it is hardened sufficiently so that it may be handled without being damaged.

DRY TO RECOAT: Time interval between application and ability to receive next coat satisfactorily.

DRY TO TOUCH: Time interval between application and tack-free time. A film of paint is ☐dry to touch" when it is hardened sufficiently so that it may be touched lightly without any of it adhering to the fingers.

DRYING: Act of changing from liquid to solid state by evaporation of volatile thinners and by oxidation of oils.

DRYING OIL: An oil that hardens in contact with air.

DRYING OILS: Oils which are converted to solids when exposed to the oxygen in the air. Linseed oil, tung oil and perilla oil are the three principal vegetable oils of the drying class. Menhaden, or fish oil, is the only animal oil of the drying class suited for use by the paint industry. See semi-drying oils.

DUCT: Round or rectangular sheet metal piping used to distribute warm or cool air from one part of a structure to another.

DULL RUBBING: Act of rubbing a dried film of finishing material to a dull finish, usually with abrasive paper, pumice stone, steel wool and oil or water.

DUST FREE: A film of paint is ☐dust free" when dust no longer adheres to it.

DWARF PARTITION: A partition short of the ceiling.

EFFLORESCENCE: A deposit of water soluble salts on the surface of masonry or plaster caused by the dissolving of salts present in the masonry, migration of the solution to the surface and depositing of the salts when the water evaporates. It often shows up as a white crystalline substance on brick fireplaces.

EGG SHELL LUSTER: Finish that closely resembles the luster of an egg shell.

ELASTIC: Ability to return to the original volume or shape after distorting force has been removed.

ELECTROSTATIC SPRAYING AND DIPPING: By this method the article to be sprayed is attached to one pole of a high voltage electrostatic field. The mist from the spray gun is given an opposite charge and thereby becomes attracted to the article. The mist travels around corners with the result that the article is coated more uniformly on all sides and with very little overspray. The same principle applies to articles that have been dipped in paint, but this time it is used in reverse for the purpose of removing excess paint. The ⊡tears" and ⊡beads" that collect at the bottom of the dipped article are repelled and fly off, leaving the article free from them.

EMBOSSED PAPER: Wallpaper run through rollers with raised areas, to provide a light relief effect.

ENAMEL: Type of paint made by grinding or mixing pigments with varnishes or lacquers.

EPOXY ESTER: Epoxy-modified oil; single package epoxy.

EPOXY RESINS: Resins obtained by condensation reaction between phenols and epichlorohydrin.

ERGONOMICS: The practice of designing machinery and furniture with an eye toward the comfort of the human using that machinery and furniture.

EROSION: Wearing away of paint films; heavy chalking tends to accelerate erosion.

ESCUTCHEON: A decorative plate surrounding any piping penetration to provide a finished appearance to a wall.

ETCH: Surface attack by chemical means.

EVAPORATION RATE: Rate of solvent release.

EXPANSION JOINT: Any separation or break in construction that allows for expansion and contraction of the materials.

EXTENDER PIGMENTS: Pigments that provide very little hiding power but are useful in stabilizing suspension, improving flow, lowering gloss, and providing other desirable qualities.

FACADE: The entire exterior side of a building that can be seen at one view.

FADEOMETER: Device for measuring color retention or fade resistance.

FADING: Reduction in brightness of color.

FASCIA: A board or band where the roof meets the outer wall, often at the outer face of a cornice.

⊡FEEL": The painter's term for the working qualities of a paint.

FILLER: Inert material used to fill or level porous surfaces, like open-pore woods such as oak and walnut.

FILM BUILD: Dry thickness characteristics per coat of paint.

FILM THICKNESS GUAGE: Device for measuring film thickness above substrates; dry or wet film thickness gauges are available.

FINIAL: The top shape of a spire, gatepost, pinnacle or other architectural point.

FIRE CRACKS: Cracks in plaster due to exposure to unusual heat during curing.

FIRE DOOR: A metal sheathed door.

FIRE RETARDANT PAINT: Paint containing substance that slows down the rate of combustion of flammable materials or renders material incapable of supporting flame.

FLAG: End of hog brush bristle which divides into two or more branches like a tree. Flagging provides brush with the ability to hold paint.

FLAGSTONE: A flat stone used for walkways and floors.

FLAKING: Detachment of small pieces of paint film.

FLASHING: Sheet metal used to cover open joints of exterior construction such as roof parapets or roof valley joints to make them waterproof.

FLASH POINT: Degree of temperature at which a flammable liquid starts to emit flammable gases.

FLAT FINISH: Dull finish, no gloss.

FLATTENING AGENT: An ingredient--usually a metallic soap, such as calcium, aluminum or zinc stearate--used in lacquers and varnishes to reduce the gloss or to give a ▢rubbed" appearance.

FLATTENING OIL: A varnish-like composition, made of thickened oil dissolved in a thinner, used to reduce paste paint to a flat paint.

FLAT VARNISH: Varnish that dries with a reduced gloss, made by adding such materials as silica, wax, or metallic soaps to the varnish.

FLAT WALL PAINT: A type of interior paint that is designed to produce a flat or lusterless finish.

FLINT PAPER: Abrasive paper which is grayish-white in color. Inexpensive but has short working life.

FLOATING: Separation of pigment colors on surface.

FLOOR VARNISH: A varnish made specifically for application to floors.

FLOWING VARNISH: A varnish that has been designed to produce a smooth lustrous surface without rubbing or polishing.

FLUE: An enclosed pipe or chimney for carrying off smoke, gas or air.

FLUORESCENT PAINT: Luminous paint which glows only during activation by ultraviolet or "black" light.

FLUTE: A concave groove or channel in columns, masonry or other architectural members.

FOOTING: Enlarged base at the bottom of a wall which distributes the weight (load); foundation for a column.

FORMICA: The trade name for plastic laminated sheeting.

FOYER: The entry area between the entrance and the main interior of a building; lobby.

FRIEZE: The decorative horizontal band near or at the top of a wall.

FUGITIVE COLORS: Tinting colors that are not permanent, but are subject to fading rapidly when exposed to light and air.

FUNGICIDE: A substance poisonous to fungi; it retards or prevents fungi growth when added to paint.

GABLE: The triangular upper end of an exterior wall.

GALVANIZE: The dipping of iron or steel in molten zinc, or electroplating with zinc.

GALVANIZED IRON: Sheet metal coated by dipping in hot zinc.

GANGWAY: A temporary footway or passageway made of planks.

GARGOYLE: A roof spout carved to represent a grotesque human or animal figure projecting from a roof scupper to carry rainwater clear of the structure.

GARNET PAPER: Abrasive that is reddish in color, hard and sharp; it comes from the same source as the semi-precious jewel by that name. It's more expensive than flint sandpaper but lasts longer.

GAS CHECKING: Fine checking; wrinkling, frosting under certain drying conditions; said to be caused by rapid oxygen absorption or by impurities in the air.

GHOSTING": A coating with a skippy appearance.

GINGERBREAD: Gaudy ornamentation in architecture.

GLAZIER'S POINTS: Small triangular pieces of flat metal used as a nail to hold glass in place while putty is being applied.

GLAZING: (Puttying)-setting glass. A process of applying transparent or translucent coatings over a painted surface to produce blended effects.

GLOSS: A term used to indicate the shine, luster or sheen of a dried film.

GLOSS OIL: A varnish composed primarily of limed resin and petroleum thinner.

GLOSS RETENTION: Ability to retain original sheen.

GRAININESS: Roughness of a protective film resembling grains of sand.

GRAINING: Simulating the grain of wood by using paint.

GRAIN RAISING: Causing short fibers on surface of bare wood to stand up by applying water. Liquids that do not raise the grain are known as non-grain-raising.

GRAVEL STOP: A strip of metal with a lip to contain the gravel around the edge of a roof.

GREEN: Unseasoned lumber, or freshly applied, unhardened concrete or plaster.

GROUND COAT: The coating material that is applied before the graining colors or glazing coat.

GROUND PAPER: Wallpaper coated with an overall background color.

GROUT: Fluid cementitious material used to cement together to fill the joints of masonry and tile.

GUTTERS: Wood or metal conveyances carrying rain water off roofs to down-spouts.

GYPSUM: A common mineral composed of hydrous calcium sulphate. Gypsum, when heated, forms plaster-of-Paris. Fabricated gypsum products used in build-ing include wallboards, plasterboards, sheetrock, etc.

HAIR LINES: Very narrow cracks in a paint or varnish film.

HANGER: Any device used to suspend and support one object from another; a tradesman who installs wallboard.

HARDBOARD: Pressure formed boards of wood fiber.

HARDENER: Curing agent; promoter; catalyst.

HARD OIL FINISH: A varnish giving the effect of a rubbed-in-oil finish but pro-ducing a hard surface. The term has gradually been extended to cover all sorts of interior architectural varnishes with a moderate luster.

HASP: The hardware consisting of a slotted arm that fits over a U shaped staple to permit the use of a padlock.

HEAVY BODIED OIL: A high viscosity oil.

HEWN: Cut with blows from an ax, chisel, or other crude instrument; roughly dressed wood.

HIDING POWER: Capacity of a paint to hide or obscure the surface on which it is applied; degree of opacity of a pigment or paint.

HIGH BUILD: Producing thick dry films per coat.

HOLIDAYS: Areas of a surface missed by the painter.

HOUSE PAINT, OUTSIDE: Paint designed for use on the exterior of buildings, fences and other surfaces exposed to the weather. HUE: A general term used to distinguish one color from another, like a red hue, yellow hue, etc.

HUMIDITY: Amount of water vapor in the air.

HYDRAULIC SPRAYING: (See Airless) Spraying by Hydraulic pressure.

HYDROUS: Containing water.

HYGROSCOPIC: Tendency to absorb water.

INERT: A product having inactive chemical properties.

INDUCTION BAKING: Using heat induced by electrostatic and electromagnetic means for baking of finishes.

INHIBITOR: Any material which would delay or stabilize a chemical reaction.

INTERCOAT CONTAMINATION: Presence of foreign matter between successive coats.

INTERMEDIATE COAT: Middle coat; guide coat.

INTUMESCE: To form a voluminous char on ignition; foaming or swelling when exposed to flame. IRON WORK: The use of iron for ornamental hardware, railings and the like.

JALOUSIES: Window blinds or shutters with movable or fixed slats, usually of glass, similar to a venetian blind.

JAMB: The finished vertical framing of a door or window.

JAPAN DRIER: Varnish gum with a large proportion of metallic (lead, cobalt, manganese, etc.) salts added to hasten drying. It is used in paints, varnishes and enamels.

JOURNEYMAN PAINTER: One who has had at least three years experience and schooling as an apprentice.

JUXTAPOSITION OF COLORS: Placing colors side by side, or close together. Complementary colors such as blue and orange in juxtaposition accentuate each other.

KICK PLATE: The strip of metal along the lower edge of a door.

KILN DRIED: Lumber which has been oven dried as opposed to air dried.

KILN DRYING: Drying of wood, paint, varnish or lacquer in a room or compartment with heat and humidity regulated.

KIOSK: A small circular or geometrically shaped structure with a dome or tent shaped roof.

LAC: A natural resin secreted by certain insects which live on the sap of trees in India and other Asian countries. Marketed in various forms; seed lac, button lac, and shellac.

LACQUER: Finishing material that dries by the evaporation of the thinner or solvent. There are many different types of lacquers, the most important being that based on cellulose nitrate. Besides the cellulosic compound, lacquers contain resins, plasticizers, solvents and dilutents.

LAMPBLACK: Pigment made by burning coal tar distillates without sufficient air. Not quite true black.

LAPPED JOINT (Wallpaper): Joint made by trimming one selvedge and overlapping the other.

LATEX: A rubber-like substance, used as a common binder for emulsion (water-based) paints. There are naturally occurring and manufactured synthetic latexes.

LATH: In plastering, the strips of wood used as a foundation for plastering.

LATTICE: The use of lath or similar lumber set in a crisscross pattern.

LEVELING: The formation of a smooth film on either a horizontal or vertical surface, independent of the method of application. A film that has good leveling characteristics is usually free of brush marks or orange peel effects.

LIFTING: Occurs when an undercoat or old paint is softened by solvents used in fresh coats of paint that follow. Usually caused by not allowing sufficient time for the undercoat to harden before applying additional coats, but can also occur due to chemical reactions between different types and quality of paints.

LIGHT WELL: An open area within the confines of a building providing air and light.

LINING PAPER: Wallpaper without a ground (overall background color), used mostly for wall conditioning.

LINSEED OIL: Vegetable oil obtained by crushing seed of flax plant. Drying properties accentuated by heating oil to 130 to 200 deg. C. to form what is known as ⬜boiled" linseed oil. Metallic salts or driers are added to increase rate of drying.

LINTEL: A horizontal structural member placed across the top of a door or window opening.

LIQUID DRIERS: Solution of driers in paint thinners.

LIQUID WOOD FILLER: Varnishes of low viscosity, usually containing extending pigments, for use as a first coating on open-grain woods. Its purpose is to afford a non-absorbent surface for succeeding coats of varnish. It is frequently colored so as to stain and fill in one operation.

LIVERING: Formation of curds or gelling. Coagulation of varnish finishing material into a viscous, rubber-like mass. Trouble is usually caused by chemical reaction of two or more products.

LOFT: An unfinished story just below the roof; large open areas within a commercial building.

LONG-OIL VARNISH: Varnish with a large percentage of oil to gum resin--usually more than 25 gallons of oil to 100 pounds of resin. Long-oil varnish is more elastic, and more durable than short-oil varnish. Spar varnish is a typical example of long-oil varnish.

MAINTENANCE PAINTING: (1) Repair painting; any painting after the initial paint job; in a broader sense it includes painting of items installed on maintenance. (2) All painting except that done solely for aesthetics.

MANTEL: The shelf above a fire place opening.

MARBLEIZING: Finishing process used to make the surface being treated look like marble.

MARINE VARNISHES: Varnishes especially designed to resist long immersion in salt or fresh water and exposure to marine atmosphere.

MASKING TAPE: Adhesive coated paper tape used to mask or protect parts of surfaces not to be finished.

MASONITE: The brand name for a hardboard product, used for siding, paneling and door facing.

MATTE FINISH: A dull surface free from gloss.

MEDIUM VALUE (Color): Color midway between a dark color and a light color.

METAL PRIMER: First coating applied when finishing metal, specially formulated to adhere to metal and resist oxidation (rusting).

MIL: Unit of thickness, 1/1000 inch.

MILEAGE: Coverage rate; square feet per gallon at a given thickness.

MILDEW: Whitish or spotted discoloration caused by parasitic fungi.

MILDEWCIDE: Substance poisonous to mildew; prevents or retards growth of mildew.

MILLWORK: All materials made of finished lumber manufactured in a planing mill, such as window and door frames, doors, panels, baseboards and the like.

MINERAL OIL: Oil obtained from petroleum by distillation or other process.

MINERAL SPIRITS: Petroleum product which has about the same evaporation rate as gum turpentine.

MISCIBLE: Capable of being mixed. Examples: lacquer thinner is miscible with lacquer; water and alcohol are miscible.

MISSES: Holidays; skips; voids.

MITER: The joining of two trim pieces at an angle.

MOBILITY: The degree to which a material flows.

MOISTURE: Finely divided particles of water.

MOISTURE CONTENT OF WOOD: The amount of water contained in wood; usually expressed as a percentage of the weight of oven-dry wood.

MOISTURE VAPOR TRANSMISSION (MVT): Moisture vapor transmission rate through a membrane such as a dry paint film.

MONOCHROMATIC HARMONY: Color harmony formed by using shades and tints of a single color.

MOPPING: Swabbing, as with roofing asphalt.

MORTISE: The cut out portion of a member, the female, cut to receive the tenon, or male portion, such as the cut out portion in a door frame to receive a lock mechanism.

MUD: In painting, the slang term for drywall taping compound.

MUD-CRACKING: Irregular cracking, as in a dried mud puddle.

MULLION: The narrow vertical bars dividing windows, or paneling.

MULTI-COLOR SPRAYING: Spraying a surface with two or more different colors at one time from one gun. The multiple colors exist separately within the material and when sprayed create an interlacing color network with each color retaining its individuality.

MURIATIC ACID: A dilute form of hydrochloric acid, used to remove efflorescence from masonry surfaces.

NEOPRENE: A trade name for synthetic rubber.

NEWEL POST: The main post at the top and bottom of a stairway supporting the handrail.

NICHE: A recessed portion of a wall, usually not to ceiling height, often housing a figurine.

NON-DRYING OILS: Oils that are unable to take up oxygen from the air and change from a liquid to a solid state. Mineral oils are non-drying oils.

NON-FERROUS: Metal not containing iron, as copper, aluminum or brass.

NON-GRAIN-RAISING STAIN (NGR Stain): Wood stain that does not raise the grain of the wood. Made by dissolving dyes used in making stains in special solvents, instead of water.

NONTOXIC: Not poisonous.

NON-VOLATILE: Portion of a product which does not evaporate at ordinary temperature.

NOZZLE: Orifice; sandblast nozzle; spray gun nozzle.

OIL COLORS: Colors ground to form a paste, in linseed oil.

OIL LENGTH: Oil length in varnish is measured by the oil in gallons per hundred pounds of resin. A long-oil varnish is tougher than a short-oil varnish. Rubbing varnish is a typical short-oil varnish and spar varnish is a typical long-oil varnish.

OIL SOLUBLE: Capable of being dissolved in oil.

OIL STAIN (PENETRATING): Wood stain consisting of oil-soluble dyes and solvents such as turpentine, naphtha, benzol, etc. Penetrates into pores of wood; has tendency to bleed.

OPACITY: Hiding power

OPAQUE: Impervious to light; not transparent.

OPEN-GRAIN WOODS: Woods of loose, open formation with minute openings between the fibers, such as oak and walnut, are called "open-grain" woods.

ORANGE PEEL: Spray painting defect, in which the coat of paint does not level down to a smooth surface but remains rough, like the peeling of an orange.

ORGANIC: Compounds produced by plants and animals.

ORIFICE: Opening; hole.

OVERCOAT: Second coat; topcoat.

OVERLAP: Portion (width) of fresh paint covered by next layer.

OVERSPRAY: Sprayed paint which did not hit target; waste.

OXALIC ACID: Type of wood bleach.

OXIDIZE: To unite with oxygen.

PAINT: An adhesive coating that is applied as a thin film to various surfaces for decoration, protection, aid to morale, safety, sanitation, illumination, fire-retarding and other purposes.

PAINT COATING: Paint in position on a surface.

PAINT GAUGE: An instrument used to measure the thickness of paint coatings.

PAINT HEATER: Device for lowering viscosity of paint by heating.

PAINT PROJECT: Single paint job.

PAINT REMOVER: A mixture of active solvents used to remove paint and varnish coatings.

PAINT SYSTEM: The complete number and type of coats comprising a paint job. In a broader sense, surface preparation, pretreatments, dry film thickness, and manner of application are included in the definition of a paint system.

PARAPET: A low wall at the edge of a roof.

PASS: (Spray) Motion of the spray gun in one direction only.

PASTE WOOD FILLER: A compound supplied in the form of a stiff paste for filling the open-grain of hardwoods, such as oak, walnut, and mahogany.

PATINA: The color and sheen achieved over time, as the greenish patina of copper.

PEELING: Detachment of a paint film in relatively large pieces. Oil base paint applied to a damp or greasy surface usually ☐peels." eventually. It is due to the new paints' inability to adhere to the substrate or coat of old paint it's meant to adhere to.

PENETRATING STAIN: Stain made by dissolving oil-soluble dyes in oil or alcohol.

PENTHOUSE: The structure on the roof of a building.

PERMEABILITY (Permeate): To diffuse through or penetrate something.

pH: A measure of alkalinity, acidity or neutrality in an aqueous (watery) solution.

PICKLING: A dipping process for cleaning steel and other metals; the pickling agent is usually an acid.

"PICK UP SAGS": When a too-heavy coating of paint has been applied and starts to sag, or run down the surface, the painter brushes up through the sagging paint to level it off.

PIER: A solid supporting column.

PIGMENT: Material in the form of fine powders soluble in oils, varnishes, lacquers, thinners and the like. Used to impart color, opacity, certain consistency characteristics and other effects.

PIGMENT OIL STAIN (Wiping Stain): Consists of finely ground soluble color pigments, such as used in paints, in solution with linseed oil, varnish, mineral spirits, etc. according to the formula being used.

PIN-HOLING: Formation of small holes through the entire thickness of a coating; see cratering.

PLASTER OF PARIS: A white powdery substance formed by calcining (heating) gypsum. When mixed with water it forms a paste that soon sets hard. Originally brought from a suburb of Paris.

PLASTICIZER: An agent added to certain plastics and protective coatings to impart flexibility, softness, or otherwise modify the properties.

POLE-GUN: Spray gun equipped with an extension tube.

"POLISHING": Said of wall paints where shiny spots or surfaces have resulted from washing or wiping.

POLYMERIC: Composed of repeating chemical units. All plastics and polymers are polymeric.

POLYVINYL ACETATE (PVA): A synthetic resin used extensively in emulsion (water) paints and wallboard primers; produced by the polymerization of vinyl acetate.

PORTICO: A roofed open space fronted with columns before an entrance.

POT LIFE: Time interval after mixing during which liquid material is usable with no difficulty.

PRIMARY COLOR: A color that cannot be obtained by mixing other colors, usually red, green, blue, and yellow.

"PRIME IN THE SPOTS": Apply a priming coat to those plaster spots that have been scraped, wire-brushed, shellacked, or have had the old paint burned off or consist of newly patched plaster.

PRIMER: Paint applied next to surface of material being painted.

"PRINT FREE": Paint sufficiently dry so that no imprint is left when something presses against it.

PROFILE: Surface contour as viewed from the edge.

PUMICE STONE: A stone of volcanic origin, which is pulverized to produce a soft abrasive used extensively in rubbing out finish coats of furniture finishes.

PUSH PLATE: The metal plate on a door, hand high.

PUTTY: Linseed oil or water based material used for glazing windows and filling nail holes.

"PUTTY COAT": Final smooth coat of plaster.

QUICK DRYING: A material with a relatively short drying time.

RAFTERS: A series of structural members supporting a roof.

RECOAT TIME: Time interval required between application of successive coats.

RED LABEL GOODS: Flammable or explosive materials with flash points below 80 deg. F. (26.7 deg. C.).

REDUCER: Volatile ingredients used to thin or reduce viscosity of a finishing material.

RELATIVE HUMIDITY: Indication in terms of percentage of amount of water vapor in a given volume of air at a given temperature, compared to total amount of water vapor the air could hold at the given temperature.

REMOVERS: Compositions designed to soften old varnish or paint coats so that they may be easily removed by scraping or washing.

RETARDERS (Lacquer): Slow drying solvents or extenders added to lacquer to delay drying of the lacquer.

"RIDE THE BRUSH": To bear down on the brush to the extent that the paint is applied with the sides of the bristles instead of the flat ends. This shortens the life of the brush.

RIDGE POLE: The highest horizontal member of a roof that receives the upper ends of rafters.

RISER: The vertical board immediately below the stair tread on a staircase.

ROLLER COATING: Process of finishing an article by means of hard rubber or steel rollers.

ROTTENSTONE: A siliceous (contains silica) limestone which when finely pulverized is used in wood finishing. It has negligible cutting action but is fine for polishing. Rottenstone is also known as tripoloi.

RUBBING OIL: Neutral, medium-heavy mineral oil used as a lubricant for pumice stone in rubbing varnish, also lacquer.

RUBBING VARNISH: A hard-drying varnish that may be rubbed with an abrasive and water or oil to a uniform leveled surface.

RUNS: Also known as ꓽsags." Irregularities of a surface due to the uneven flow and build-up of drying paint.

RUST: Rusting of metal is generally explained as an oxidizing process where oxygen from air combines with iron to form a metallic oxide; water combines with oxide to form rust.

RUST-INHIBITIVE WASHES: Solutions that etch the metal and form a dull gray coating of uniformly fine texture, thus producing a rust inhibitive surface receptive to a priming coat.

SAGS: See runs.

SANDBLAST: Blast cleaning using sand as an abrasive.

"SAND DOWN": Remove the gloss of an old finish and smooth it prior to refinishing.

SANDING SEALER: A lacquer used as a seal coat over a filler. Generally given some filling action by adding inert substances.

SASH: The framing that holds the glass in a window or door.

SATIN FINISH: Term used in describing dried film of paint or other finishing material which does not have a full luster, but a dull luster like that of satin.

SCALDING: Finish condition in which pieces of the dried finishing material come off, exposing the surface below.

SCRATCH COAT: The first coat of stucco or plaster.

SCRIBE: The cutting of the edge of one member in an irregular line so as to fit it snugly against another.

SCUPPER: An outlet or receptacle that allows water to drain from a roof, often connected to a downspout.

SEALER: A liquid coating composition, usually transparent, such as varnish, that also contains pigment for sealing porous surfaces, such as plaster, preparatory to application of the finish coats. Wood floor sealer is a thin varnish.

SECONDARY COLORS: Colors made by combining primary colors. For example, the secondary color orange is obtained by mixing red and yellow.

SELF-CLEANING: Term used to describe paint in which the rate of chalking is controlled so dirt on the surface will be washed away with accumulated chalk.

SELF PRIMING: Use of same paint for primer and for subsequent coats. The paint may be thinned differently for the different coats.

SEMI-DRYING OILS: Oils that "dry" to soft, tacky film. The principal semi-drying oil used in the paint industry is soybean oil.

SEMI-GLOSS: Sheen on a dry finish that is about half way between dead flat finish and full gloss.

SERRATED: Notched, or toothed on the edge.

SETTING UP: Initial drying of a coating to a point where it is no longer able to flow.

SETTLING: Initial drying of coating to the point where it is no longer able to flow.

SHADE: Degree of color obtained by adding black to a color or hue.

SHADOWING: When preceding coats show through the last coat, the finish is said to be "shadowing."

SHARP LUSTER: A very high gloss.

SHEET METAL: Thin metal, usually galvanized iron, used in the manufacture of gutters, ductwork, and corrugated siding.

SHELF LIFE: Maximum interval in which a material may be stored in usable condition.

SHELLAC: Resinous material commonly known as flake shellac; secreted by insects. Shellac is obtainable in two forms--orange and bleached. Used as a furniture finish and to seal in bleeding knots on wood.

SHIM: A thin piece of wood or metal used to level or align another member.

SHOP PRIMED OR SHOP COATED": Said of a prefabricated article that has been primed at the factory.

SHRINKAGE: Decrease in volume on drying.

SILKING: A surface defect characterized by parallel hair-like striations in coated films.

SILL: The horizontal member at the bottom of a door or window.

SINGLE ROLL: A single roll of American-made wallpaper is a roll containing 36 square feet of paper. Wallpaper usually comes in bolts which contain two or three single rolls.

SKIN: A tough layer or skin formed on the surface of a paint or varnish in the container. Caused by exposure to air.

SKIPS: Uncoated spots on finished surface.

SKIRT (APRON): The horizontal member under a window stool.

"SLIP UNDER THE BRUSH": When coating materials are easy to apply, this is sometimes said of them.

SLOW DRYING: Requiring 24 hours or longer before recoating.

SLURRY COAT: A thin, watery material composed of sand and cement commonly applied by brush.

SOFFIT: The underside surface of an arch, cornice or other subordinate member of a building.

SOLVENT: A liquid capable of dissolving a material is said to be a solvent for the material.

SPACKLING COMPOUND: A kind of plaster that is used to fill surface irregularities and cracks in plaster, wallboard, and wood. This compound, when mixed with paste paint, makes what is known as Swedish putty.

SPALLING: The cracking or slaking of concrete, often caused by the swelling from rusting reinforcing bars beneath the surface.

SPAR VARNISH: A very durable varnish designed for severe service on exterior surfaces. Such a varnish must be resistant to rain, sunlight and heat. Named for its suitability for the spars of ships.

SPATTER FINISH: Finish which provides a spattered or spackled effect.

SPLASHBOARD: A horizontal member placed on an edge fastened to a wall above and on top of a sink top or drain board.

SPOT REPAIR: Preventive maintenance; repainting of small areas.

SPRAY HEAD: Combination of needle, tip and air cap.

SPRAY PATTERN: Configuration of spray, gun held steady.

SPREADING RATE: Amount of area a given volume of coating material can be spread over by spraying, brushing or other method of application. Spreading rate is generally indicated by square feet covered per gallon.

STAIN (WOOD): Finish for wood containing a dye or pigment. Stain sinks into fibers of wood to a certain extent while paint and lacquer ordinarily do not penetrate wood.

STEAM CLEAN: A cleaning process using live steam.

STEEL WOOL: Steel in fine strands. Comes in grades 3,2,1,0,2-0,3-0, and 4-0 (finest).

STIPPLE FINISH: Finish obtained by tapping surface with stipple brush or rolling out using appropriate roller cover, before paint is dry.

STILE: The vertical framing member of a paneled door or paneling.

STOOL: The flat horizontal member at the bottom of an interior window.

STOOP: The broad platform step at the entrance of a house.

STORM WINDOW: A window placed outside an existing window as a protection against weather.

STORY: That portion of a building between any floor and the floor above.

STRAIN: To filter, and remove impurities from the paint or varnish.

"STRETCH": The width of the area on which a painter will normally apply paint across a ceiling or down a side wall from one set position.

STRIKING IN: Materials used in finishing are said to "strike in" when they soften undercoats and sink into them.

STRINGER: The sloped outside member supporting a stairway.

"STRIP": Complete removal of an old finish with paint removers.

STROKE (Spray): A single pass in one direction.

STUD: The vertical member supporting a wall.

SUBSTRATE: Surface to be painted.

SUCTION SPOTTING: Spotting of paint job caused by oil in new coat being absorbed by spots or porous areas of surface.

SUNDAYS: Places skipped when applying finishing materials to a surface.

SURFACE DRYING: Drying of a finishing material on top while the bottom remains more or less soft.

SURFACER: A paint used to smooth the surface before finish coats are applied.

SWEDISH PUTTY: See spackling compound.

SYNTHETIC RESIN: An artificial resin or plastic produced by systematic exploitation of chemical reaction of organic substances.

TACKINESS: Stickiness. When a painting material dries out, gels or sets up, it loses tackiness, or stickiness.

TACK RAG: Cloth impregnated with varnish used in wood finishing to remove abrasive dust from surface of wood, before applying finishing materials.

TENSILE STRENGTH: Resistance to elongation; the greatest longitudinal stress a substance can bear without rupture or remaining permanently elongated.

TERRACOTTA: Baked clay and sand masonry units, normally more intricately molded than brick; a brownish-orange color.

TERTIARY COLORS: Colors made by combining colors on the color wheel that are adjacent, like red and orange.

TEST PATTERN: Spray pattern used in adjusting spray gun.

TEXTURE PAINT: A heavy bodied paint that may be manipulated by brush, trowel or other tool to give various patterns.

THINNERS: Volatile liquids used to lower or otherwise regulate the consistency of paint and varnish.

THRESHOLD: A doorsill.

"THROUGH DRYING": Uniform drying of the entire paint film.

THUMBNAIL PROOF: Checking hardness of a finish by pressing thumbnail against it.

TINGE: Slight trace of color.

TINT: A light value of a color--one made by adding white to the color.

TITANIUM DIOXIDE: White pigment used extensively in paint making. Comes in two forms, rutile and anatase. It is chemically inactive and is not affected by dilute acids, heat or light.

TONE: A graduation of color, either a hue, a tint, or a shade; as a gray tone.

"TOO MUCH DRAG": Refers to paint that has excessive "pull" or "drag" in its application.

TOOTH: Roughened or absorbent quality of a surface which affects adhesion and application of a coating.

TOUCH-UP PAINTING: Spot repair painting usually conducted a few months after initial painting.

TOXIC: Poisonous.

TRANSOM: The hinged glazed window opening over another window or door providing ventilation; horizontal crossbar in a window, over a door, or between a door and window above.

TRELLIS: A structure of lattice work.

TRIM ENAMEL PAINT: Surface coating differing from ordinary house paint by faster drying, by having more gloss and showing fewer brush marks. Used mostly on trim, shutters, screens.

TURPENTINE: Colorless, volatile liquid having a characteristic odor and taste. Obtained by distillation of the oleoresinous secretions found in living and dead pine trees.

TWO-COAT SYSTEM: Two-coat paint application for initial painting.

UNDERCOAT: Second coat in three-coat work, or first coat in repainting.

UNDERTONE: A color covered up by other colors but when viewed by transmitted light, shows through the other colors modifying the effect.

VACATIONS: The uncoated portion of a finished object. Also known as "skips" and "holidays."

VALUE: Term used to distinguish dark colors from light ones. Dark values are known as shades; light values as tints.

VAPOR BARRIER: Any material used to retard the flow of vapor or moisture into walls.

VARNISH: A liquid composition, which is converted to a translucent or transparent solid film after application in a thin layer.

VARNISH-STAIN: Interior varnish tinted with pigments or dyes.

VENEER: A thin layer of expensive hardwood glued to a less expensive wood or a thin layer of marble or brick covering a material for a wall.

VERANDA: An open porch usually roofed.

VESTIBULE: An entry anteroom, sometimes used as a waiting room.

VISCOSITY: Internal friction of a fluid that influences its rate of flow to change or form the thickness of a paint product before application.

VOLATILE: Said of a liquid that evaporates.

WAINSCOT: The paneling on the lower part of a wall; lower portion of a wall finished differently (with paint, wallcovering, etc.)

WALLBOARD: A composition sheet material used for covering walls and ceilings, a substrate for plaster such as sheetrock.

WALL BOARD: Term refers to such boards as pressed cellulose fibers, plasterboard, cement-asbestos board, and plywood, all used in place of plaster on interior surfaces.

WALL SIZE: Solution such as glue, starch, casein, shellac, varnish or lacquer, used to seal or fill pores of wall surfaces to stop suction, counteract chemicals or stains and prepare surface for paint, paper or fabric.

WARM COLORS: Colors in which red-orange predominates, as opposed to cooler blue-green colors. This term is applied because of the association with fire, heat and sunshine.

WARMING COLORS: Any color except green may be "warmed" by adding red. Green is warmed by adding yellow.

WATER BLASTING: Blast cleaning using high velocity water.

WATER CLOSET: A small room with a flushable toilet.

WATER STAIN: Stain soluble in and mixed with water.

WEATHERSTRIP: The process of applying thin strips of metal and felt to cover the joints between a door or window and its jamb, casing or sill, to keep out air, dust or rain.

WEEP HOLES: Openings left in walls to permit drainage.

"WET EDGE TIME": The length of time before a "stretch" of paint sets up without showing lap marks when the painter applies the next "stretch."

WIRE BRUSH: A hand cleaning tool comprised of bundles of wires: also the act of cleaning a surface with a wire brush, including power brushes.

YELLOWING: Development of yellow color or cast, in whites, on aging.

ZINC CHROMATE (Zinc Yellow): Metal priming pigment with important rust-inhibitive properties.

APPENDIX

HOUSE PARTS MAP

flashing
shingles
dormer
flashing
rafters
partition
porch post
facia or cornice board
header
cased opening
stair rail
stair tread
stair riser
stair stringer
Post or column
bridging
floor joists
plaster arch
mantle
hearth
flashing
roof boards
rafters
lath
plaster
ridge board
ceiling joists
window header
window sash
window sill
gable rake molding
cornice return
gutter
drip cap molding
shutters
basement sash
window area-way
grade line
wood sub-floor

WINDOW PARTS

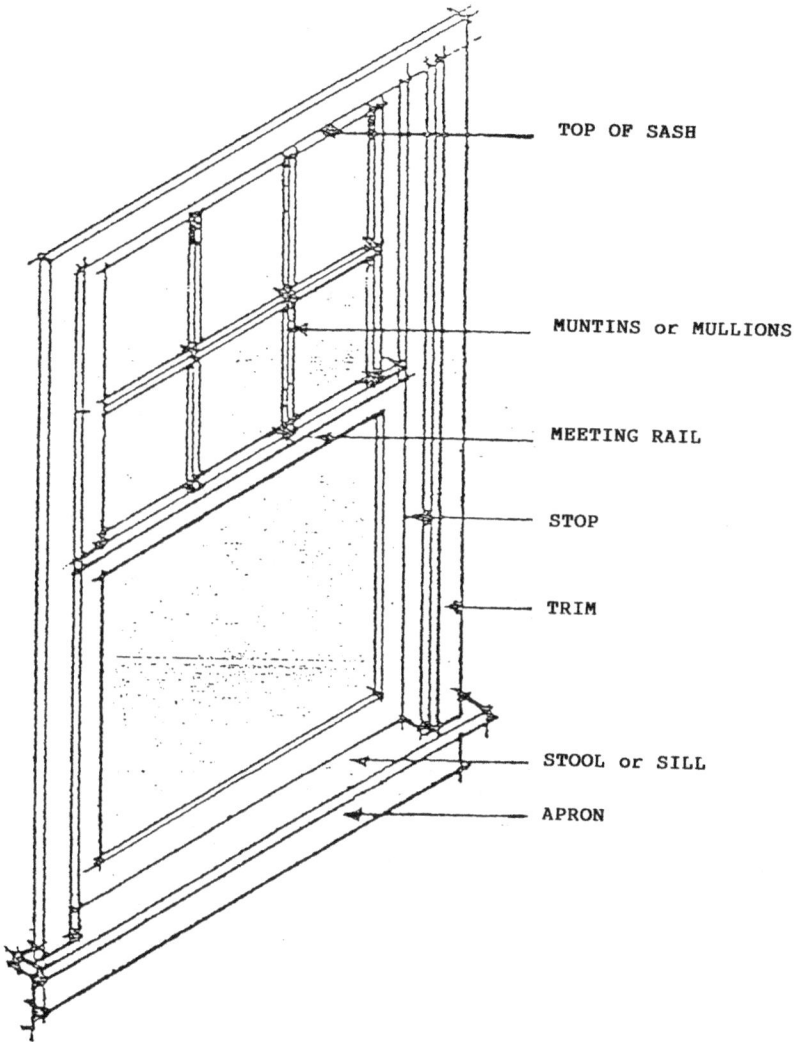

TOP OF SASH

MUNTINS or MULLIONS

MEETING RAIL

STOP

TRIM

STOOL or SILL

APRON

PAINT MECHANIC - READY FOR WORK

Allen Wrench set
Broom
Brush - large steel wire
Brush - small brass wire
Brushes - oil 4", 3", 1"
Brushes - latex 5", 3", 1"
Brushes - artist
Buckets - 2 gallon & 5 gallon
Caulk
Caulking gun
Drop Cloths - Interior (New)
Drop Cloths - exterior
Dust masks
Dusting brush
Electrical adaptor - 3 prong to 2
Extension cord
Extension poles
Garden hose nozzle
Goggles
Fix-all
Glazing compound / Putty
Gloves - rubber
Hack Out Knife
Hammer
Hardware storage boxes
Hose - 25'
Joint compound
Knife - broad 12"
Knife - Flex blade putty 2"
Knife - Broad 4"
Knife blades - utility
Knife - utility (retractable)
Knife - chisel blade (scraper)
Knife - 5 in 1
Ladders - 6' step
Marking pen
Metal file
Nail sets

Paint thinner
Paint can opener
Paint remover
Paint strainers
Paint pail ladder hooks (2)
Pencil
Plastic - 2 mil
Pliers - slip joint
Rags
Razor scraper
Razor blades - single edge
Respirator - dual cartridge
Roller handles - 7" & 9"
Roller covers - 7" & 9"
Sandpaper - assorted grades
Scrapers
Screwdriver (#2 phillips head)
Screwdriver (#1 phillips head)
Screwdriver (1/4"slotted head)
Screwdriver (1/8" slotted head)
Scrub brush - Exterior
Spackle
Sponges
Steel wool - 00
Stir sticks
Tack cloths
Tape - masking (blue)
Tape - electrical
Tint rack
TSP
Vacuum
Wallpaper scoring tool
Window opener saw
Z prime